COOKING LIKE MUMMYJI

COOKING LIKE MUMMYJI
VICKY BHOGAL

illustrations by Kate Miller

photographs by Mark Luscombe-Whyte

SIMON & SCHUSTER
A VIACOM COMPANY

First published in Great Britain by Simon & Schuster UK Ltd, 2003
A Viacom Company

Simon & Schuster UK Ltd
Africa House
64–78 Kingsway
London
WC2B 6AH

3 5 7 9 10 8 6 4 2

Design: Jane Humphrey
Copy editor: Deborah Savage
Typesetting: Stylize Digital Artwork

Printed and bound in China

ISBN 0 74323 982 2

THE SECRET TO COOKING LIKE MUMMYJI

Our home food is much simpler than the food you find
in Indian restaurants. We use very few spices.
The same ingredients are generally used for everything but,
like musical notes, can be combined in many different ways
to create beautiful melodies.

The main element missing from restaurant food is the female energy.
The kitchen is always the best place to be in an Indian
or British-Asian household. Full of women joking, laughing,
gossiping, confiding, moaning about their mother-in law
or daughter-in-law – they do all this whilst cooking
and this is the magic ingredient, which cannot be replicated.
The wisdom, love and culture of these women rubs off from
their hands into the food to give a special taste.
This is why two Indian women who start off with the same ingredients,
following the same method, never produce the same results.
It is this alchemy, turning the simplest ingredients into gold,
which you will learn by making the recipes in this book.

Dedicated to my parents, who, through their sacrifices,
have taught me the sheer necessity of trying to fulfil all your dreams
and have given me the courage to reach for the stars.
Thank you for absolutely everything.

On previous pages, from left to right: Pooiji (my aunt), Bhabiji (my cousin's wife), me, Choti Pooiji (younger aunt)

On opposite page, clockwise from top left: me and my Mum; my sister, Karen; Karen blowing out birthday candles; my brother, Aneil; Inderveer, my cousin's elder son; *Papiji* (my Grandad), me and my Dad; Jasneal, my cousin's little son; *Pooiji* (my aunt) and *Choti Pooiji* (younger aunt); *Pooiji* (aunt) and *Phupherji* (uncle). *In the centre:* my Mum and Dad

contents

VICKY INTRODUCES HERSELF

I was drying up the dishes in the kitchen when the doorbell rang. It was a particularly blustery and sodden Saturday in April, the kind of grey day when all you want to do is shut out the dreariness and dozily curl up in the warmth of the living room. I was at my parents' house in Norfolk for the weekend, a welcome break from the relentlessness of life in London. My Pooiji and Phupherji (Dad's older sister and her husband) had arrived from Derby. They had endured a three-hour journey through twisting country roads to bring us ladoo (Indian sweets) to celebrate the birth of their second grandson, Jasneal.

After we had all had some elaichi chaa (cardamom tea), my Mum and I set about making roti (the evening meal). I was making a tarka (the onion-and-garlic base for a sauce) and my eyes were still moist from the sting of the onions. My Mum and Pooiji were enjoying an animated conversation at the kitchen table. My Pooiji got up and peered into the pan; with a wide-eyed enthusiasm like that of a young child about to impart a great secret, she turned to me and said in Punjabi, 'Vicky, do you know how to make this really delicious? Sprinkle a tiny bit of zeera (cumin) in at this stage and it will make all the difference, trust me.' Blinking back tears, I turned to grab the jar of cumin.

We started talking about recipes and methods we had both tried and then she said, 'It is such a shame that so many Indian girls of your age don't know how to cook or share your enthusiasm. Nowadays, girls are either so busy studying or they just have no interest. Gone are the days when they used to stay in the kitchen by their mother's side and were able to cook for the whole family by the age of ten. Now it's "I'm going here," or "I'm going there," or "I've got exams!" Soon, no-one will be able to cook proper roti anymore and we elders will be fed chilled supermarket chicken biryanis, a twinpack of frozen naan and a jar of mango chutney!'

I thought about this long and hard that evening. The conversation had left me with a deep sense of sadness. I lay in bed and thought about how times had changed. Was the culinary future bleak for my generation?

In previous generations, girls in India had no other fate but to help their mothers with the cooking and cleaning from the moment they could walk (unless, of course, they were very rich). They did not step out of their homes in the villages and their daily routine revolved around mealtimes. They stayed at their mother's side, carefully watching as each spice was added to the magic mix, as rice was washed of its milky starch, as roti (bread) was effortlessly puffed up on the thawa (cast-iron griddle) and as deft fingers gently placed pakore (vegetable fritters) into hot oil bubbling hungrily away. By the time they had reached double figures they could measure quantities with the naked eye; cook seven dishes simultaneously; chop piles of onions without shedding a single

tear; roll **rotis** that were all exactly the same size; use their bare hands as human tongs, plunging them into open flames to flip rotis over; and – like a salwar-kameez-wearing, unflinching David Blaine – emerge without a single burn.

All this in preparation for their years of marriage. Back then high-quality marriage offers came to girls who were of good family, had fair skin, were young, could provide a substantial dowry, and could cook delicious food. Women wanted their daughters to be knowledgeable in all matters of cooking and household duties, so they would hopefully not receive quite as much grief from their mother-in-laws, or bring shame upon their own mother for failing to teach them well.

With my parents' generation, things began to change. Some of them were born in this country whilst the rest came over as children or teenagers. Their parents came here blinded by the promise of a life of prosperity. England was a dream destination the land of the Raj, the heart of the Empire, **Wilait**, England. It seemed to offer hope and modernity. They were wooed by myths that this was a land where every man who stepped off a ship onto England's pebbly shores could become an umbrella-carrying gentleman and amass wealth beyond his dreams. In fact, my father clearly remembers that, when he was young in India, he would endlessly wish to visit this magical place.

Left to right: my cousin Sukhmanie, me, my *Choti Pooiji* and my big *Pooiji* (my two aunts), my *Bhabiji* (my cousin's wife)

It was as though the streets were paved with gold and, like brown-skinned Dick Whittingtons, families gathered their belongings and embarked upon their adventures.

From here on, families suffered from the conflict of trying to remain true to their traditional values and customs and having to adapt to their new way of life in England. Going back would mean failure and many had nothing to go back to, having sold what they had to finance following their dream.

Although a lot of the girls who came over as children or were born in this country around that time stayed at home and got married by the age of eighteen, it became increasingly clear that to survive here, you needed education. Education was quickly seen as the means by which to achieve dignity and equality. Even for girls. Over time families increasingly needed the daughter or daughter-in-law to contribute to the family income. The higher the education, the higher the salary brought in through the front door.

Today's ideal bride is still a girl who is fair and beautiful and from a respectable family, but now she needs to be just as good kicking butt in the courtroom or performing a triple by-pass as she is at making perfect crispy *samose*. Talk about being a superwoman.

Therefore my generation grew up with a huge emphasis on education and with constant homework to do. We were still expected to help out with household chores and cooking, but it was a tiny amount in comparison with generations gone by.

My generation also grew up with a sense of rebellion and a greater need to fit in with the surrounding culture. Freedom became a desire and the word was often regarded by our parents as an expletive with its connotations of unruly Western ways — not at all appropriate for well-brought-up Indian girls. Often, after a number of battles, strict parental rules were relaxed a little and some girls were able to go shopping with appropriate female friends, watch films at the cinema with appropriate female friends, and visit appropriate female friends' houses to watch videos (but not stay over). Learning how to cook featured low on the list of priorities.

But the expectation that girls ought to be able to cook remains. Mothers-in-law still despair when daughters-in-law can't cook and mothers still worry about their daughter's ease of life after marriage. Cue endless nagging because, even though they want you to be an A* student, old priorities still run deep and can occasionally rear their disapproving heads.

That evening in April I arrived at the conclusion that there must be a way to resolve this so that everyone is happy. Many British-Asian girls are simply put off by the thought of standing in the kitchen for years until they know the recipes backwards and the measurements have become innate. Indian mothers do not use measurements, you see. (By the way, when I refer to British Asians I mean those who were born here such as myself. When I refer to Indians or Indian things I mean all that originated in the motherland.)

Once, when I was in my early teens, I asked my mother how much salt was needed for a dish I was half-helping her to prepare. She replied, 'We don't use measurements. That's for English people. We don't do things that way. If you stand here long enough and cook it over and over again, you will soon learn how much salt to put in.' That was the point where I began to be put off. I just wanted to know how to make it, not move permanently into the kitchen at the sacrifice of 'Top Of The Pops' and listening to New Kids On The Block in my bedroom.

Years later when I went to university I thought I had learned enough to get me by, but I craved my Mum's food. There were many dishes I hadn't learnt and the ones I could vaguely cook weren't a patch on what they should be. So I learnt to cook properly, and practised. Some girls at uni did not know how to cook. At weekends they would often bring back a week's supply of their Mum's food packed into foil containers ready for the freezer. When I showed some of them how to cook in my final year, they marvelled at how simple it was and exclaimed, 'Why couldn't my Mum have explained it as simply as that?' Often they scrambled to find a pen to write recipes down.

Remembering these times led me to a light bulb moment. The old methods of learning are becoming impractical. Wouldn't it be great if there were some sort of fun guide which tells you exactly how to make everything just like our mothers do? A book which could teach you dishes from scratch but one you could also refer to if you're stuck, if you have, say, forgotten the measurement of masala or *haldi*? Like, for example, when you have relatives over, or have just gotten married, or are in halls and would give your laptop away for a plate of *pakore*.

So on the morning of that Sunday in April I decided that I was to write this book so that Indian girls get to keep their lives and grades but also manage to dazzle their families with their culinary skills.

But this is not just a book for other British Asians. I have often thought it such a shame that the Western world is not let in on the secret of real Indian home-cooking, as though it is a sort of long-standing trick, our last remaining jewel. I have cooked for many people and my friends have always been amazed by how different the food is from restaurant food, that it has all been cooked fresh from scratch without any artificial ingredients and that it is so healthy. There is much less oil involved than restaurant food and it is quite mild. They always demand to know why they have never tasted such food before. In fact, a few of my friends hated 'curry' but, after a cautious forkful of my food, have proclaimed themselves fans of Indian cuisine. They are always interested to know how to make the dishes and never fail to be shocked at the simplicity and speed with which they are rustled up. A proper Indian meal provides the perfect balanced meal, based on ancient *ayurvedic* principles and is all you need to keep energy levels up and fat levels down. And it is much more interesting and delicious than steamed alfalfa sprouts with a shot of wheatgrass.

It is high time we opened the door to let non-Asians into our secrets. It is not fair to have denied them, albeit unintentionally, for so long. Therefore, this book is also an insider's guide to the truth of our food so that you may share in our love of it. It will teach you recipes handed down from our ancestors in India, the authentic techniques, the real names and how to pronounce them. You'll be impressing your friends in no time. Just remember to eat with your right hand, using a piece of the roti as a scoop, for that authentic experience.

The Indian cookbooks I have read tend to fall into one of two categories. They are either geared towards the British curry-house fan, full of dishes no self-respecting Indian would ever cook or eat at home (and tend to be written by non-Asians), or they are the type that target real food-lovers and contain recipes which, although delicious, are highly stylised and often complicated. They often contain dishes from restaurant kitchens in India, rather than the traditional food cooked at home in this country.

Left to right: me, my sister Karen, Dad, my brother Aneil, Mum

Whenever I attempted to cook any of the fancy dishes from those books, they were often received with quizzical looks and I would get a word in my ear about cooking food 'the way we make it'.

In this book there are no silly ingredients or overly complicated techniques. This is just the way **Mummyji** makes it. I am from a Sikh family so a lot of the dishes and names are Punjabi, but in general this is the way a lot of British Asians cook their food. A lot of the dishes overlap the religious boundaries.

Although real Indian cooking is instinctive and has no measurements, I have of course included them. I have used the simplest measurements possible so you don't have to buy lots of new equipment or be fiddling around with various bits and pieces in the kitchen — a definite sign that your methods are inauthentic.

After you have tried the dishes even once, you will begin to get an instinct for how much of the spices to add to suit. The recipes are just a guide to get you started; it is important to allow them to become your own creations. You may decide you prefer a bit more chilli or garlic or want to add different vegetables or use different meat. You may come up with your own serving and presentation ideas.

As this book is specifically about the food we British Asians have grown up eating — and not food from the Indian subcontinent — I found it impossible not to include the variants on English food our parents invented to make use of the ingredients readily available at the local supermarket. These dishes are immense fun and demonstrate the Indian take on English food. They were often created for the children when they returned home from school in the evenings. I have also added recipes that have evolved through the influence of Italian, Chinese and Mexican food around us. These dishes are given an Indian twist for extra impact.

So, these are in essence the reasons why I decided to put this book together. The more I thought about it, the more it made sense and, of all the ambitions I've ever had (namely to meet the Dalai Lama, guest star on the US show 'Angel', win Pop Idol, be in a dance chorus in an Indian film, overcome my fear of dogs and grow another four inches), this was the one I felt most passionately about, and maybe could actually do. I just love food you see. It is my obsession. I love reading about it, cooking it but, most of all, eating it. My friends get alarmed at how, despite my 5-foot-4-inch frame, I can pack away the same quantity of food as two firemen. I could eat all day, dish after dish, and sometimes have. My sister is always concerned about how much I think about food, that I plan my evening meal whilst eating breakfast, that sometimes I cannot choose between two main courses and have both. My mother is concerned I'll balloon and never get married. But I just love food. I eat and cook food of all nationalities but Indian food is where my heart is.

Sikh gentleman shopping in a Southall supermarket

I hope this book will be a tiny glimpse into the reality of Indian food. I hope it eliminates some of the misconceptions. British-Asian life is vibrant and rich and I hope this book will open your eyes to some of that. For British Asian readers, they will recognise themselves in parts of it and will be able to recreate the food their family upbringing revolved around. For non-Asian readers it will be the start of a new adventure.

I wanted this to be a real family affair so you will encounter many family members along the way too. For in truth, they are the experts. They are the real Dons of the cooking after decades of experience and I am just the humble messenger who loves the results. All in all, I hope that you will now be able to spice up your life.

With lots of love,

Vicky

BEFORE YOU BEGIN

In order to make an authentic meal, you need to start off with the correct equipment and ingredients. Don't worry, you don't need to buy a thousand different spices and expensive pots and pans, but there are a few things that are absolutely necessary such as a thawa, garam masala and haldi. It is a good investment to make a trip to your nearest Indian grocery store to buy these items, even if it is once a year, as both utensils and ingredients are a fraction of the price they would be in mainstream supermarkets (assuming they stock them). Once you have these core items, the remaining ingredients are very easy to come by.

I have also included other valuable information you will need before you begin cooking, such as tips and techniques to make the recipes even easier: like guides for preparing and freezing ginger and how to cut onions in your hands. There is also a guide to metric and imperial weight equivalents for some of the main ingredients. After you read this section, you should be armed with all the knowledge you need to cook like Mummyji.

You'll find that words in Punjabi are in a different typeface (like this) and you can look them up in the glossary on page 41.

UTENSILS AND EQUIPMENT

Large saucepan with a lid It is best to use a large stainless-steel saucepan with a lid (even better if it has a see-through lid). Non-stick pans with black coating make it difficult to see the true colour of the spices and therefore you run the risk of not cooking for the correct length of time. Large pans are best as often a lot of water is added or sauces bubble up and therefore need the room.

Frying pan This is often needed for making a tarka and is therefore very important. Choose a good-quality, heavy, large pan.

Thawa This cast-iron flat griddle has a large black flat-plate and a long tapering handle. Seek one out at an Indian store; they are very inexpensive and absolutely vital for making rotia – a large frying pan will never create the results you want. Wash gently with a soapy sponge after using, making sure any burnt bits of roti are removed, but do not use a wire wool brush on it. Always preheat it before cooking on it.

Tongs Long, flat tongs will prove indispensable when turning over rotia and are also useful for dropping items such as karele into the deep-fryer.

Madhua This tool is a wooden disc with a long wooden handle and is available from Indian stores. It is vital for making *saag* as it pushes and presses the leaves. If you really cannot find one, use a large good-quality potato masher instead.

Rolling pin This is used to roll out all the breads, so make sure you get a good-quality wooden one: you'll be using it a lot!

Chopping board Small round wooden chopping boards are sometimes used to roll the breads out on, instead of on the work surface. They are especially good for *makhi di rotia*. My Dad also uses one of these to cut meat on.

Tablespoons and teaspoons The simplest of measurements. Make sure you get a measuring spoon set, they are very inexpensive.

Mini-blender This will save you an awful lot of time and will prove to be a Godsend. They are not very expensive and you can whizz tomatoes, onion and chillies up in seconds. Get a mini one for this purpose and a larger one for making drinks.

Sharp knife Very important for cutting up vegetables. Be careful with your fingers.

Colander A must for draining vegetables and meat before adding to the pan. Line with kitchen paper and also use it to drain snacks straight from the deep-fryer.

Wooden spoon Traditionally women use a *karchhi*, which is a large metal spoon, for mixing but, as these scrape against the pan and become hot, it is better to use a large wooden spoon with a long handle instead.

Wooden spatula This is important when making some delicate rice dishes and fish as, unlike a spoon, you can gently move the ingredients around without breaking them.

Fish slice This is used for turning over *parathe*, turning over snacks as they deep-fry and much more.

Large perforated spoon Get one with a long handle with a wooden or plastic section at the top, so your hands will not get hot. This large perforated metal disc is perfect for making *bhoondi* and also for dropping *pakore* and other snacks into the deep-fryer.

Slotted spoon Use this to remove deep-fried snacks from the oil and also to add and remove ingredients from pans during cooking.

Pestle and mortar These are great for smashing up spices such as cardamom pods for tea.

Tin opener Well, wouldn't get very far without one of these now, would we?

Measuring cups These are very inexpensive and are available from most supermarkets. They are a very simple measurement to use until you get used to measuring by eye.

Kitchen paper Use to drain fried snacks and also place between the lid and pan during steaming process in some dishes.

Baking dishes A basic utensil for any dishes that need to be baked in the oven.

Aluminium foil Use a good-quality foil for covering dishes to be cooked in the oven or for keeping *rotia* warm.

Deep-fryer A lot of families just have a large metal deep pan, which they fill with oil to deep-fry. An actual deep-fryer is safer as you can regulate the temperature. Never leave unattended, not even for a second.

Coffee grinder Use this to grind up all your garam masala.

BASIC INGREDIENTS

These are all the core ingredients you need to make simple dishes. Keep these in your cupboards at all times and you will be able to rustle up delicious food at any moment.

SPICES AND OTHER FLAVOURINGS

Black pepper Peppercorns in a mill are much better then the ready-ground versions. You can then remove some peppercorns and smash in the pestle and mortar if a recipe calls for cracked black pepper or simply grind with the mill for finer pepper.

Cumin seeds Often fried at the beginning of the cooking process, these give a warm flavour and a pungent aroma. They have digestive properties and release flavour upon heating.

Garam masala This is the most vital ingredient. This ground spice blend of coriander seeds, black peppercorns, cumin seeds, cassia bark, brown cardamom, bay leaves and cloves is used in almost everything we make, even some desserts! Either make your own (see page 197), which will give you more than enough for six months, or buy a good-quality Indian brand from an Indian grocer's. Keep in a cool, dry, dark cupboard.

Light malt vinegar Dark malt vinegar has too strong a taste but this adds just the right level of sourness to many sauces.

Salt Use a good-quality salt and keep some coarse sea salt too.

Turmeric, ground A member of the ginger family, this bright yellow powder is mostly used to add colour and a touch of flavour. Don't use too much or it will give a bitter taste. It is this that sometimes makes your fingers yellow when eating Indian food. Again, buy a good-quality Indian brand from an Indian grocer's and store in a cool, dry, dark cupboard.

FRESH VEGETABLES

Coriander, fresh This wonderful green leaf is packed with aromatic flavour and is often added both during cooking and also at the end. This is actually very important – it has been drummed into my head since I was about eight years old! The coriander sprinkled on top at the end of cooking is in no way merely a pretty garnish but adds the final element of flavour too. Any Indian home dish served without this would be considered incomplete. Not only would it look shoddy, aesthetically unpleasing and as if you haven't made an effort, it would also taste wrong. By omitting this part you may cause offence to Indian guests and may as well not have bothered cooking the dish at all. We keep a very large bag of frozen chopped coriander in the freezer and the act of grabbing a handful and sprinkling over the top of a cooked dish is almost a reflex and takes seconds. See page 32 on how to prepare and freeze coriander so you always have it to hand.

Garlic Strong in flavour, this is often used alongside onions in the frying stage. See page 36 on how to peel and cut garlic.

Ginger Fresh root ginger is used frequently to give heat and a delicious flavour; it is very good for you too. See page 32 for how to prepare and freeze ginger for easier use.

Green chillies, fresh We generally use green chillies in most of our food as they give a milder taste than red. See page 32 for how to prepare and freeze these.

Onions Onions are the base ingredient of a *tarka* to create the sauce for the dish and are therefore needed at all times.

Tomatoes We occasionally use fresh tomatoes but mostly it is the canned variety, with their slightly sour taste, that is the staple of our sauces. Buy whole plum or chopped canned tomatoes as indicated in each recipe (it depends upon what texture is needed). These can be bought very inexpensively so it is worth always keeping a couple of cans in the cupboard.

Potatoes These are used in many recipes, mostly as the secondary vegetable. They are a good basic to have at all times.

STORECUPBOARD AND FRIDGE/FREEZER BASICS

Frozen mixed diced vegetables Keep a bag of these in the freezer as they can be used in many ways; from rice dishes to a speedy alternative for fresh vegetables in a dish.

Oil Which oil you use is up to personal preference but do not use virgin or extra-virgin olive oil as it burns. Popular choices are sunflower, rapeseed, vegetable or mild olive oil.

Rice Always use a good-quality Indian brand basmati rice and never short-grain or any other types.

Roti flour Indian grocers sell very large bags, which could last you a long time. Smaller packets are available from most supermarkets. Choose from white, brown or wholemeal wheat flour as you prefer. My family uses wholemeal.

Yogurt Good for the digestive system and quite a staple, natural, low-fat, set yogurt is eaten nearly every mealtime and goes with everything. It is an essential part of the meal, creating a balanced diet, and is essential for counterbalancing the chillies in dishes. We mix it thoroughly with enough milk until smooth, though some families eat it quite runny. It is also used in cooking as a souring agent. See page 196 for making your own yogurt. Most supermarket natural yogurts are quite sweet, but fine nonetheless. Visit Indian grocers for the live, sourer yogurt which we often use.

MORE SPECIALISED INGREDIENTS

Once you have the basics, buy and add these ingredients as you wish so that you are able to elaborate the dishes.

SPICES AND OTHER FLAVOURINGS

Achaar mix (panch-puran) Packets of these seed mixtures are available from Indian grocers. *Panch* means 'five' and here are the five spices: fennel, cumin, onion, fenugreek and mustard seeds.

Asafoetida Tiny quantities of this strong spice are used in some dishes.

Bay leaves These give a soft, deep flavour to sauces.

Cardamoms, brown These are larger and have a deeper flavour than their green counterparts. Smash and add to sauces and tea, but do not eat.

Cardamoms, green Stunning to the eye; these pods are used in many dishes and also tea to impart its distinctive bittersweet flavour. They have quite a heady bittersweet slightly perfume-like aroma. Again, do not eat them.

Carom seeds This is an intense and pungent spice that becomes very aromatic once heated. It is often used whole and its taste is hot and slightly bitter, not dissimilar to that of thyme.

Cassia bark These pieces of bark have a sweetish, incense-like, woody, musky aroma, a bit like trees just after it has rained. They add a distinct flavour to sauces and desserts.

Cinnamon Thinner and smoother than cassia bark, it has a slightly more savoury taste.

Cloves Used whole in many sauces and desserts, these give a strong flavour and scent.

Coriander seeds Warm and fragrant, these have a mild taste.

Dried mango powder Unripe green mangoes are peeled and sun-dried in the Indian sunshine and then finely ground to add a tangy fruitiness to sauces and snacks.

Dried red chilli flakes These are very fiery and give plenty of zest and flavour to snacks and sauces.

Fennel seeds Hugely aromatic, these seeds are often used for pickling and in making tea.

Fenugreek, dried Sold in packets, this is quite dissimilar to fresh *methi* and is added dry to snacks. Some packets recommend using in the place of fresh *methi* by soaking in water but I prefer to use fresh leaves.

Fenugreek seeds These little brown seeds are usually used as a pickling spice, although they are also used for making the *khadhi* sauce. They impart a very strong flavour and scent.

Mustard seeds, black These tiny black seeds are heated to give off their particular flavour. Bengalis grind them into a paste and often use it to cook fish.

Pickled chillies Sold in jars in supermarkets, these are technically Middle-Eastern but give a wonderful salty, sour heat when chopped.

Pomegranate-seed powder Made from crushed pomegranate seeds, this powder gives a fantastic sweet and sour taste that is perfect for fillings and fried snacks.

Saffron Famously the most expensive spice in the world, saffron is used sparingly to add a golden colour and a delicate sweet flavour.

Tukmaria seeds Also known as *sabja* seeds or grains basilic. Tiny black seeds, supposed to have a cooling effect on the stomach. They swell up when soaked and are very commonly used in *falooda*.

Tandoori masala powder This dark red powder is made from coriander, red chilli, cumin, black pepper, ginger, cardamom, bay leaves, fenugreek, garlic, cloves, salt and a little oil. It gives a rich, deep spiciness and slightly sour taste when added in a very small quantity to sauces. Used in a marinade, it gives that delicious flavour which makes tandoori chicken such a delight.

STORECUPBOARD INGREDIENTS

Food colourings (green, red, yellow) Use these pretty powders to colour rice (see page 150).

Corn flour/Polenta This corn flour comes in coarse and fine varieties. It is best to get both, as recipes often require them to be combined. This flour is used to make breads and to thicken *saag*.

Gram flour This flour is made from ground pulses very similar to chick-peas. It is widely used for making batters for snacks.

Palak Spinach leaves, which are often sold puréed in large cans as a base for *saag* (see page 193).

Pomegranate syrup Added to milk, this dark pink, sticky, sweet liquid gives a powerful flavour.

Rose-water This fragrant water is added to desserts and drinks for an angelic touch.

Rose syrup Thicker than rose-water, this adds a stronger flavour.

Semolina Semolina is widely loved when turned into a very sweet dessert.

Sevian Thin vermicelli noodles are available at supermarkets to make a dessert with.

Coconut cream You can buy this in cans quite easily from the supermarket. Make sure it is white, thick and creamy. It is used to create a creamy sauce and to pacify chilli.

Sultanas, green Green sultanas can be bought from Indian grocers and are smaller, greener and not as sweet as golden ones. If you can't get hold of them, though, golden ones are fine instead.

Tamarind You can buy blocks of this compressed sour fruit, to which boiling water is added, to make a tamarind water to add to sauces or make into a chutney. Be sure to remove the stones when it has dissolved.

PULSES

Thomi mahaar dhal These are split urid beans with their skins removed, leaving a creamy textured, white dhal that has a mild flavour.

Saaf di mahaar dhal These are small cylindrical beans with black skins covering creamy white interiors. The strong earthy flavour is derived from the skins.

Chana dhal (split chick-peas) This is a very common Indian dhal. These split yellow peas are small and sweetish in flavour.

Moong dhal (whole mung beans) These shiny green oval beans are very nutritious and are easy to digest.

Masoor dhal These split red lentils are the popular salmon-coloured ones found in most supermarkets. They have a delicate flavour and produce a lovely yellow dhal when cooked. They cook quickly and are thus cooked in a pan rather than in a pressure cooker.

Saaf di masoor dhal (whole brown/green lentils) These round flat lentils range in colour from brown to khaki green and are readily available everywhere.

Moth dhal (whole moth beans) These are brown cylindrical beans and are often added to other *dhala*.

Rongi dhal (dried kidney beans) These shiny, deep red, dried kidney beans produce a hearty dish when combined with other *dhala*.

Kale chole (dried chick-peas with skins) These are small, rust coloured dried chick-peas with their skins still on.

Mahaar dhal 2-pieces (split urid beans) These are given this name as the beans are split, but not skinned, creating a black-and-white effect. Some recipes require the skins to be mostly removed by rinsing, but others retain the skins to add to the flavour.

FRIDGE INGREDIENTS

Butter Use a good-quality butter where referred to and never, ever margarine.

Ghee This clarified butter is often used for frying breads, as it does not burn easily like butter. See page 32 for how to make your own.

Paneer This milky, firm Indian cream cheese comes in blocks and is now starting to appear on supermarket shelves. Eat cooked, not raw.

FRESH VEGETABLES, FRUIT AND NUTS

Almonds Often used in flaked form, these milky nuts give a creamy sweetness to desserts, rice and sauces.

Fenugreek, fresh This richly flavoured leaf is often added to vegetables and breads. See page 32 on how to prepare and freeze fenugreek.

Lemons or limes Used to sour sauces, though some families use citric powder instead. Keep fresh lemons and limes in the fridge and also a bottle of lemon juice in the cupboard.

Mustard leaves, fresh Look for these at an Indian grocers or check when they are next coming in so you can make the traditional Punjabi *saag* (see page 193).

Pistachio nuts These green nuts add flavour and colour.

Red chillies, fresh Much stronger than green chillies, these are rarely used in cooking but look fantastic for presentation.

Tinde Indian baby pumpkins; these little green vegetables are available from Indian grocers. They can be chopped and frozen.

Karele Bitter gourds, available from Indian shops and some supermarkets.

Mooli This long, white radish can be peeled, sliced and eaten raw with salad or grated and used as a hot filling.

SHOPPING, PREPARATION AND COOKING TECHNIQUES AND TIPS
SHOPPING AND STOCKING UP

Buying spices Only buy good-quality Indian brands from an Indian grocer's. Even if you only make a special car journey once a year it will be worth it, as the ingredients are of a much better taste, are a fraction of the price that they are in supermarkets and you will find a better range. Plus a friendly smile of course!

Freezing ginger Ginger is used a lot and is a main ingredient in almost every *tarka*. Therefore you need it close to hand and it is helpful not to have to keep buying it fresh and prepare it from scratch every time.

Buy 450 g (I lb) of fresh root ginger. Peel and then grate it all into a large bowl. Shape into teaspoon-sized balls and freeze in a large bag. Whenever you need ginger for a *tarka*, you simply reach into the freezer and drop a ball or two straight into the pan.

Freezing coriander Coriander is also always needed and defrosts easily on contact. Buy about four large bunches and wash thoroughly. Holding tightly, use a sharp knife to chop finely (including the stalks). Place into large bags and freeze. Break off a handful straight from the freezer whenever needed and sprinkle straight on to food.

Freezing chillies Always remember to wash your hands after handling chilli or it will be a trip to the A & E department when you have red raw eyes. Buy 450 g (1 lb) of green chillies and remove the stalks. Grind one finely in a blender and see how much one chilli constitutes (it should only be a few flakes). That is your guide. Grind the rest of the chillies and freeze in ice-cube trays. Turn out the cubes when frozen, place in a large bag and keep in the freezer. One whole ice cube of chilli is about 8–9 whole chillies. Slice off the required amount when needed with a sharp knife.

Freezing fenugreek It is always a good idea to have some of this to hand in the freezer. Buy four bunches of fenugreek leaf. Wash thoroughly. Remove the leaves and discard the stalks. Chop finely with a knife or in a blender (you want fine pieces though, not purée). Place in a bag and freeze.

Making ghee Try using this clarified butter when frying breads as it doesn't burn and leaves the bread crisp. Here's how to make your own. You can make a smaller quantity if this sounds like more than you'll need.

Shoppers in a fantastic Indian supermarket in Southall

1 Melt 2.25 kg (5 lb) of butter in a pan and bring to the boil, stirring all the time.

2 Leave to simmer for 30 minutes.

3 Take off the heat and skim off all the scum at the top.

4 Leave to cool in the pan for about a couple of hours.

5 Place in a jar and discard any solid salt in the bottom of the pan.

6 Cover and store in the fridge. It will keep for one year.

PREPARATION

Size of vegetables, fruit, eggs, etc This is always medium-size, unless 'small' or 'large' is specifically stated in the ingredients list.

Washing ingredients One of the things my mother instilled in me was to always wash meat before cooking, to clean it thoroughly and pick off excess fat, even if it is packed as ready to go (such as skinned and diced chicken). Years ago, I made some meat on the bone without washing and it was noticed as little bits of blood and skin remained. Quite unpleasant. We usually wash cut meat, fish or vegetables before doing anything else and leave them draining in colanders until it is time to add them to the sauce.

Measuring ingredients Indians and British Asians rarely use scales; traditionally, ingredients are measured by eye but it takes a long time to learn to do this. One of the simplest ways to measure ingredients (until you're able to visualise quantities) is in spoons or cup measures, depending on the amount, and this is the way ingredients have been specified in this book as far as possible.

A standard measuring cup holds 250 ml (8 fl oz). This means that three-quarters of a cup is 175 ml (6 fl oz), half a cup is 125 ml (4 fl oz) and quarter of a cup is 50 ml· (2 fl oz). Solid ingredients as well as liquid ones can be measured in spoons or cups and where this is done, the volume is always for the prepared ingredient, e.g., '½ cup chopped pistachios' means you need to chop as many pistachios as needed to half-fill the cup, not measure half a cup of pistachios and then chop them.

The table opposite gives some equivalent metric and imperial weights to 1 cup of some common ingredients.

MEASURING COMMON INGREDIENTS BY CUP

1 cup of roti or gram flour...125 g (4½ oz)

1 cup of uncooked basmati rice..225 g (8 oz)

1 cup of granulated sugar...250 g (9 oz)

1 cup of raisins...150 g (5½ oz)

1 cup of chana dhal (split chick-peas).......................................200 g (7 oz)

1 cup of moong dhal (whole mung beans)...................................200 g (7 oz)

1 cup of masoor dhal (red split lentils)......................................200 g (7 oz)

1 cup of saaf di masoor dhal (whole brown/green lentils)................200 g (7 oz)

1 cup of saaf di mahaar dhal (whole urid beans)..........................200 g (7 oz)

1 cup of moth dhal (whole moth beans)....................................200 g (7 oz)

1 cup of rongi dhal (dried kidney beans); kale chole (dried chick-peas with skins).......200 g (7 oz)

1 cup of thomi mahaar dhal (washed, split urid beans)..................200 g (7 oz)

1 cup of mahaar dhal 2-pieces (split urid beans).........................200 g (7 oz)

1 cup of coarse semolina..200 g (7 oz)

1 cup of coarse corn flour (polenta)...175 g (6 oz)

1 cup of fine corn flour (polenta)...125 g (4½ oz)

1 cup of natural yogurt..250 g (9 oz)

1 cup of butter...250 g (9 oz)

1 cup of peas/sweetcorn kernels...125 g (4½ oz)

1 cup of frozen diced mixed vegetables.....................................150 g (5½ oz)

1 cup of canned chopped tomatoes..225 g (8 oz)

1 cup of halved cashews...125 g (4½ oz)

1 cup of chopped pistachios...125 g (4½ oz)

1 cup of shelled, mixed nuts..125 g (4½ oz)

1 cup of flaked almonds..100 g (3½ oz)

1 cup of peeled cooked prawns...150 g (5½ oz)

Cutting vegetables in your hands Indians don't actually use chopping boards for vegetables (they use them for meat though, of course). Cutting vegetables in my hands was one of the techniques I had to learn quite young. It means that, often, you can be cutting one thing whilst keeping an eye on another. Usually, the item is held in the palm of the left hand and carefully cut with a sharp knife in the right. Although I would get funny looks if I started using chopping boards, you should maintain safety at all times.

Cutting onion Usually, it is topped and tailed and the skin is peeled off. It is then cut in half lengthways. Using a sharp knife, it is cut (but not right through to the other side) at small intervals down lengthways and then down widthways (creating a criss cross). You then take the knife and slice right across the onion at small intervals widthways. Tiny little squares should fall away.

Peeling and cutting garlic Garlic peel is very sticky so the best way is to take the flat edge of a large knife and press on to the clove of garlic until you hear a crunch. The skin should now just peel away in one go. Take the clove of garlic and, very carefully, cut at small intervals down widthways and then once down the middle lengthways (but not right through) creating a criss cross. Then cut across very finely so that tiny squares fall away.

Rinsing dhal before cooking Dhal always need to be checked over for stones before cooking, although nowadays many *dhala* are very clean. They then need to be washed to remove dust. Traditionally, *dhala* are washed and rinsed about 10 times. Place the dhal in a saucepan and, using warm water, rinse the dhal. The water will become foamy. Use your hands to wash the dhal and rinse with more warm water until the water begins to run clear. Some *dhala*, such as *masoor*, will be difficult to rinse until the water runs completely clear – so about 10 rinses is sufficient.

You can sometimes buy packets of dhal in Indian grocers labelled 'washed', but this only means the skins have been removed; they still need rinsing.

COOKING

Cooking a tarka This refers to the stage consisting of frying the onion in oil with a variety of other ingredients (depending upon the recipe), such as garlic, ginger, chillies, garam masala, salt, coriander, turmeric powder and other spices. This creates the base for the sauce and is the most essential part of the cooking process. If this part is not done correctly, the whole dish will be ruined. A basic *tarka* is as follows:

1   Heat the oil (do not add ingredients to cold oil in a pan, as this will give an unpleasant flavour).

2   If frying cumin, only fry for a couple of seconds until sizzling – cumin burns easily so keep a close eye.

3   Add the chopped onion and garlic. Almost always use finely chopped garlic as opposed to crushed as this gives a better flavour – crushed garlic is too strong.

4   If the onions are to be blended in a mini-blender then keep them soft and white; otherwise, fry until golden brown for vegetables and deep golden brown for meat dishes (check the individual recipes). If the onions are not cooked properly the whole dish will have a weak taste. But do not burn! Unless the onions are to be blended, make sure they are finely chopped otherwise they will not melt into the sauce and you will have pieces of onion floating around.

5   When golden, reduce the heat and wait for a minute or remove pan from the heat. This is so when you add the tomatoes, it doesn't splatter everywhere. Stir the tomatoes in and then return to the hob, keeping the heat low.

6   Quickly add the other ingredients – ginger, chilli, coriander leaf, salt, turmeric and garam masala – and stir well.

7   Now this is the vital part of the *tarka* stage. It is referred to as **raara**. Keep on a low heat and cook for about 5–10 minutes until the mixture has become very shiny and the oil has separated. Keep stirring throughout, adding splashes of water if it becomes too dry. Press the onions into the tomato mixture to get an even sauce. Only when the mixture is shiny with the oil clearly separate do you add the next ingredients. This stage is so important as the onions are blending into the sauce, the spices are cooking and releasing their flavour, the tomato is getting fully cooked, the ginger is melting down and all the flavours are binding together. If you are hasty with this stage you may as well forget the whole thing. The secret to fantastic Indian food lies in getting this right. Patience is a virtue, remember!

Flipping over roti Be very careful with this, as it is very delicate. Hold right at the very edge with the tongs. Be very gentle with it as it is puffing up on the flames, giving it a nudge with the tongs to flip over to the other side.

Adding water to sauces Always add boiling water to dishes that are being cooked. This is because the mixture is already hot and adding cold water will upset the balance of temperature. It will also take longer to bring to the boil and therefore the dish will take longer to cook. Adding boiling water saves time so boil it first in the kettle

Cooling down sauces with too much chilli We eat yogurt with our meals to counter-balance chilli. If you have put too much in your dish, add a little cream to sooth it down or a touch of sugar. Add these ingredients slowly, tasting as you go. Do not drink water if you have eaten a mouthful of food burning with chilli – water will simply disperse it and make it worse. Have a spoonful of sugar (Mary Poppins style) or yogurt to cool down.

Getting rid of excess salt Take a potato or two, peel and cut into small chunks. Add these to the dish you are cooking with a little water and bring to the boil. Simmer for 20 minutes and then take out the potato and discard. The potato should soak up the excess salt.

Thickening a sauce If your sauce is too watery, take off the lid and boil on a high heat, stirring occasionally to check thickness.

Thinning a sauce If your sauce is too thick, add boiling water, stir and simmer gently.

If a sauce sticks If you find that your meat or vegetables are sticking to the bottom of the pan, do not scrape the stuck-on residue off. Simply add a splash of water, turn the heat very low and cover. The steam will lift it all away.

Ventilation Always remember to have the extractor fan and the windows open when cooking Indian food to get rid of excess smells. You don't want the smell of frying onions wafting around or sticking to your sofa.

Making dough Add water very slowly in small amounts. When kneading, make sure to knead hard with your right fist, pressing in with the flat of your knuckles. Then fold the mixture and knead again. Repeat until firm. A good roti dough should keep in the fridge for 5 days. If it goes slimy and dark before then, discard. It means that you made too soft a dough. Use less water next time and knead for longer.

What to do if a paratha has gone hard If your plain paratha goes rock hard it is due to one of two reasons. Either you used too little dough (use a larger ball next time) or the thawa was on too high a heat. It must be on a very low heat.

Wrapping roti Keep rotia warm and moist by wrapping in foil or a clean tea towel as soon as you cook each one until ready to be eaten.

Cooking rice Always wash rice before cooking: put it in a saucepan and rinse it until the cold water runs clear, as this eliminates the starchiness that causes the stickiness.

Treat cooked rice gently. Never, ever stir or plunge a spoon straight into cooked rice to take a portion. Before serving, always take a fork and lightly graze the surface of the rice to loosen the grains. Work your way through the pan, shaking off any rice that sticks to the fork, so that you have singular grains. Only then should you very gently use a spoon or spatula to take a portion and place on a plate.

GLOSSARY OF PUNJABI TERMS

Various Punjabi words are used throughout this book (though generally English is used in ingredients lists and methods, except where no suitable translation exists). If any term is unfamiliar, just look it up here.

achaar *(a-chaar)* pickle

adrak *(adh-rahk)* fresh root ginger

ajwain *(joo-weyn)* carom seeds

Akhand Path continuous recitation of the **Guru Granth Sahib** for 48 hours

aloo *(a-loo)* potato

aloo gobi potato and cauliflower

aloo paratha fried bread stuffed with potatoes

amchoor *(aam-choor)* dried mango powder

anardhana *(anaar-dhaana)* pomegranate-seed powder

atta *(a-taah)* wheat flour

Auntyji term of respect for an older, unrelated female

badaam *(ba-dhaam)* almonds

barri elaichi *(barr-rhee lejji)* large brown cardamoms

belan *(bel-un-aah)* rolling pin

besan *(be-suhn)* gram flour/chick-pea flour

Bhabiji brother's or cousin's wife

bhajis deep-fried onion balls eaten as snacks

bhangra Punjabi folk music, now set to modern beats and very popular in British-Asian youth culture

bhati *(bhat-ee)* frying pan

bhatura/bhature deep-fried bread(s), made with milk

Bhenji older sister or female cousin

bhoondiwala dahi gram flour balls in yogurt (recipe on page 180)

biryani baked rice dish

chaat popular south-Indian snack, often with potatoes and tamarind

Chachiji aunt (Dad's younger brother's wife)

chakla *(chak-uhl-aah)* small round wooden chopping board

chamche *(chaam-che)* spoons

My cousin, Papa Paaji, holding a tray of garam masala whole spices

chana dhal split chick-peas

chappal sandal

chaul *(chorl)* rice

chimta *(chim-taah)* tongs, for turning **roti** during cooking

chole chick-peas (referred to as **chana/channe** in other dialects)

Choti Pooiji younger aunt on Dad's side of the family

dahi *(da-hee)* natural yogurt

dalchini *(dhaal-chee-nee)* cassia bark or cinnamon

desi anything traditionally Indian or when a British-Asian person feels like behaving in a traditional, Indian way instead of in a modern, Western way (acting *desi* means going back to your roots and old values)

dhaak sultanas

dhala *(dhaala)* pulses

dhalwala paratha fried bread with lentils (recipe on page 164)

dhaniya *(dhun-ee-ya)* coriander leaves

dhaniya daana *(dhun-ee-yaa-dhaan-aa)* coriander seeds

Diwali Hindu festival of lights

elaichi *(lejji)* green cardamoms

falooda milkshake-style dessert of ice cream and **sevian**

gajar carrot

gajarela carrot halva (recipe on page 211)

gandha *(gahn-dhaa)* onion

garam masala *(gah-rum ma-saa-la)* indispensable blend of powdered spices (recipe page 197), often referred to as just **masala**

ghee clarified butter

gram flour chick-pea flour also known as **besan**

Guru Granth Sahib Sikh holy book

Gurudwara Sikh Temple

haldi *(huhl-dee)* ground turmeric

hari mirch *(ha-ree-mirch)* fresh green chillies

hing *(heeng)* asafoetida

imli *(im-il-ee)* tamarind

jalfrezi Indian restaurant dish containing peppers

kale chole dried chick-peas with skins on

kali mirch (kaa-lee-mirch) black pepper

Karah Parshad sweet distributed as a grace at the *Gurudwara*

karchhi traditional large metal spoon

karele bitter gourds

kasoori methi (kah-soori-me-thee) dried fenugreek

keema minced meat

kesar (khe-sarr) saffron

khadhi potatoes and onions in a gram flour, yogurt and fenugreek sauce
   (recipe page 190)

kofte meatballs

laal mirch (laal-mirch) red chillies

lahsun (lahh-sun) garlic

Langar meal eaten at the Sikh Temple

lassi (la-see) yogurt drink

laung (lohng) cloves

luhn (loohn) salt

madhua (ma-dhoo-aah) wooden disc-shaped utensil with handle, for
   pressing saag

mahaar dhal 2-pieces split urid beans

makhan butter

makhi di atta (ma-khee-dee-a-taah) corn (maize) flour, i.e. polenta

makhi di roti corn flour bread (recipe on page 163)

Mamma/Mammaji uncle on Mum's side

masala a spicy thick sauce (as in Lamb Chop Masala) or term for recipes
   where a mixture of spices has been used to pep them up, e.g. Masala
   Burgers, i.e spicy burgers (this term has quite broad meanings but it
   generally means 'spicy', not to be confused with 'hot' as in chillies)

masoor dhal/masoora di dhal red split lentils

Massi/Massiji aunt on Mum's side

mattar peas

methi (me-thee) fenugreek leaves

methi daana (me-thee-dhaan-aa) fenugreek seeds

moong dhal whole mung beans

moth dhal whole moth beans

Mughal dynasty from Persia that ruled India in C17th and C18th, giving name also to certain style of north-Indian food

Mummyji Mum

naan leavened bread cooked in a **tandoor**

Naniji nan or grandmother

nimbu lemon or lime

Paaji older brother or male cousin

pakora/pakore gram flour vegetable fritters

palak spinach

palhe lentil balls

panch puran *(paanch-poo-ran)* blend of 5 pickling spices

paneer soft cheese

Papiji grandad

paratha/parathe fried bread(s)

pathila *(pa-thee-lah)* saucepan

phulke bread cooked on naked flame so it puffs up

Phupherji uncle (husband of aunt on Dad's side of the family)

piaj *(pee-aaj)* alternative name for onion

pindh village; in this country, often used in the context of discussing which village your family comes from in India.

pindhus a British-Asian slang term, an amusing mild insult used for those people who are not modern or Western in their ways. They have often just arrived in Britain from India and have strong accents or old-fashioned ways and appearance or sometimes it is just used for those who are quite traditional and not very 'hip'.

pista *(pis-thaa)* pistachio nuts

Pooiji aunt on Dad's side of the family

poori(a) deep-fried crispy bread(s)

raara the stage in cooking a **tarka** when the oil separates from the spices

rai daana *(rai-dhaan-aa)* black mustard seeds

rongi dhal dried red kidney beans

roti the name of the bread more commonly known as a chapatti, roti is also a generic term for an Indian meal

saaf di mahaar dhal whole urid beans

saaf di masoor dhal whole green or brown lentils.

saag green leaves and spinach cooked in a particular way (recipe pages 72 and 193).

sabji/sabjia athough this term refers to vegetable (and occasionally some fish) dishes, which have been cooked in the appropriate way, it also means raw vegetables.

samosa/samose deep-fried triangular filled pastry

sarson (sa-rohn) mustard leaves

saunf fennel seeds

sev crunchy noodles

sevian (se-vee-aan) vermicelli

sharbart refreshing drink with ice

sirka (sir-kaah) light malt vinegar

suji (soo-jhee) semolina

sukki laal mirch (soo-khi-laal-mirch) dried red chilli flakes

tamatar (tam-aa-taar) tomatoes

tandoor clay oven used for cooking breads and some meat dishes

tandoori any food cooked in a tandoor

tandoori masala spice blend used for tandoori dishes

tarka base for sauces (see page 37)

tej patta (tehj pathha) bay leaves

tel (thayl) oil

thali stainless-steel food tray used to serve Langar

thari This is the name given to a quite runny sauce.

thariwala with a runny sauce

tharwala dahi cucumber yogurt dish (recipe on page 175)

thawa (tha-vaa) cast-iron griddle for cooking roti

thomi mahaar dhal washed, split urid beans (recipe on page 94)

tikka a diamante tikka is an adornment worn in the centre of the hairline with a pendant resting on the forehead (chicken tikkas resemble these little pendants)

tinde Indian baby pumpkins

tukmaria seeds added to desserts. They produce a cooling effect on the stomach. Also known as sabja seeds.

zeera (jee-raa) cumin seeds

(choh-tee-moh-tee-cheej)

choti

mhoti cheej

SOMETHING SMALL

SAMOSE

Indian and British Asian people do not have starters, that is a western thing, so *choti mhoti cheej* simply means 'something small' that is, snacks.

These sensational triangular pastries are amongst my most favourite things in the whole world. When I left home at eighteen to go to university, I was sure that, as these are so popular, I would have no trouble finding ready-made alternatives that could compete successfully in the taste-stakes. Not so. Of all the *samose* I have tried, and believe me, I have gobbled my way from little takeaway huts in Leicester to grand restaurants in the capital, and everything in between, not a single one was a patch on these little babies. My Mum's *samose* have a unique light and aromatic filling – softly spiced nuggets of potato, slivers of translucent onion and shimmering juicy green peas, offset by just the right amount of green chilli to add a little bite, encased in a golden crispy pastry to form little treasure chests. There are no heavy spices, excess food colouring or powdered chilli to mask the natural flavours of the vegetables, just a touch of garam masala and cumin to keep the taste fresh. We usually make these for parties and special occasions – especially Christmas. And when we do make them, my sister Karen and I eat them 24/7, for breakfast with ketchup, for lunch with *imli* chutney (page 179) and *chaul* and for dinner with *chole, palhe* and salad. We have a spat about eating an equal number each and always resort to fisticuffs over the last one.

You can make a large batch and freeze them raw; then all you have to do is take them out of the freezer and deep-fry (we have never gotten that far though as we just decide to fry and eat them all!).

I believe the most important ingredient in a samosa is laughter. The method truly does lend itself to that extra magical ingredient. They should not be made in a rush as the joy is in sitting around a table and making them with your nearest and dearest. We get a little production line going – my sister glues the edges, my Mum forms the cones and I fill them (although I sometimes end up filling my mouth with the mixture and get a slap from my Mum!). All the energy created sitting around the table, talking and joking with messy sticky hands, filters into each and every one and culminates in your mouth with that first piping-hot mouthful.

You can experiment with fillings (my cousin, Nina Bhenji, makes lovely white cabbage and sweetcorn ones) and use chicken, lamb mince or even prawn. Do remember to make the pastry though and not cut corners by using filo pastry, it never tastes the same.

Me making *samose*

4 whole, unpeeled potatoes

1½ cups frozen peas

rapeseed oil, for deep-frying and making dough

1 large onion, halved, halved again lengthways
   and then sliced thinly widthways

1 tablespoon cumin seeds

1 tablespoon salt

1 tablespoon garam masala

a handful of chopped fresh coriander

2 green chillies, chopped finely

4 cups plain flour

1 Place the potatoes in a pan of boiling, salted water and cook until soft (check by prodding with a sharp knife). Drain and rinse the potatoes in cold water. Peel the skin off with a knife and remove any darkened areas of the potato.

2 Roughly chop the potatoes into a large mixing bowl. Do not be too meticulous about this, as the potatoes will be mashed anyway.

3 Add the frozen peas to a pan of boiling water and simmer gently for about 3 minutes. Drain well and add to potatoes.

4 Place 20 ml (1 tablespoon + 1 teaspoon) of rapeseed oil into a frying pan. This part is extremely important − all the way through the cooking process of *samose* you should only ever use the oil in which you are going to deep-fry them eventually, so that the textures and flavours remain consistent. You cannot mix any oils. I am using rapeseed oil here, as it is healthy and light in taste.

5 Once the oil is heated, add the onions to the pan. After about 30 seconds, add the cumin seeds.

6 Gently fry the onions until they are translucent and the brown colour of the cumin seeds has slightly rubbed off on to the onions. The onions should not be golden but still white, just softened and translucent. Add the onions to the potatoes and peas.

7 Now add the salt, garam masala, coriander and the chillies.

8 Mix with a fork to blend all the ingredients together, very lightly mashing the potato but not too much as you still want small pieces of potato and not a smooth paste. Cover and leave to cool in the fridge for at least 30 minutes. A couple of hours would be ideal.

9 Now make the pastry. Take 1½ cups of plain flour and place in a large mixing bowl with a pinch of salt.

10 Using the rapeseed oil again, add 1 tablespoon plus ½ teaspoon of oil to the flour. Mix with fingers and combine to a dough with cold water. Do not make the dough too soft. Add the water by running your hand under the cold tap and catching a little in your cupped hand, instead of pouring water in, to ensure that you do not add too much and

end up with a sticky mess. Add water like this until you see the dough coming together in one mass. Then knead well with wet hands until the dough no longer sticks to your hands and just gives way. Cover and refrigerate for at least 15 minutes (place in a container and cover with a lid if you are planning to make the *samose* in more than 15 minutes time; cover the bowl with kitchen paper if you are making them in 15 minutes time).

11 Mix 1 cup of plain flour in a bowl with enough cold water to make a thick, sticky paste. Try to get the lumps out but do not make it too thick or runny. This will be your glue to hold the *samose* together.

12 Now we need to get everything ready to hand as timing is very important and you will not have time to be fiddling around in a drawer looking for things. Rinse the *thawa* and put it on a very low heat. Take the dough out of the fridge and place the container on the worktop next to the *thawa*. Place next to it 2 tablespoons of the rapeseed oil in a little bowl with a teaspoon in it. Place a clean tea towel that has been folded in half widthways on a plate. Get out a small sharp knife. Put the remaining plain flour on a large plate or chopping board. Get a large clean plate.

13 Take two ping-pong-ball-size balls of the dough. Dip them both in the flour and roll them both out to the size of saucers. Make sure they are both the same size.

14 Take one of the discs and dip in the flour. Shake off excess. Place flat on the work surface. Using the teaspoon, spread ½ teaspoon of the oil on the surface of the disc and sprinkle with a little of the flour (about 1 teaspoon). Place the other disc on top and lightly press edges flat to seal. Turn over and press again.

15 Dip both sides in flour, shaking off excess, and roll out to the size of a pancake. Keep dipping in flour if necessary – it mustn't stick. The pastry must be very smooth and cannot have any creases in it. It needs to be flat and even so it splits cleanly.

16 Pat off excess flour and place on the *thawa*. Cook for 3 seconds on each side and then transfer to the plate. Fold in half and cut a tiny slit at the halfway mark on the edge. Open out and cut in half. Very slowly and carefully peel the two layers apart of each half. You should be left with four semicircles of pastry. Open the tea towel and place the pastry immediately on the tea towel on the plate. Cover with the other half of the tea towel to keep warm.

17 Repeat the pastry process until you have 12 semicircles. Make sure they are covered.

18 Take one of the semicircles of pastry (keeping the rest covered until needed) and, using your middle finger, put some of the 'glue' all around the edges of the side that looks more cooked. Hold the semicircle with the straight edge facing upwards and fold

the outer left hand corner down towards the middle of the curved edge (but do not let it touch the curved edge). Bring the right hand corner down and seal where they both meet, overlapping slightly. You should be holding an upside-down cone.

19 Turn the cone the right way up and, holding it gently, fill with the potato mixture (but not right to the top). Seal the curved edges at the top together with your fingers so that the line where the samosa is sealed runs straight down the middle, adding more glue if necessary. Gently pat to even out the mixture inside.

20 When they are all filled, heat the rapeseed oil for deep-frying to about 170°C or until a little bit of the pastry rises to the surface immediately it is dropped in. Gently add the *samose* and deep-fry until golden brown and crisp, turning with a perforated spoon. Drain on kitchen paper and serve.

Matthia

(ma-teeh-aa)

CAROM-SEED PASTRIES

I usually eat these at relatives' houses or with the morning tea at the *Gurudwara* during weddings. They are best enjoyed simply on their own with a mug of steaming tea. Crumbly like biscuits, these circular pastries flake when you bite into them. They are flavoured with intense, pungent whole carom seeds, which are very slightly bitter and not dissimilar to the taste and aroma of thyme.

This is a very traditional method, which involves kneading with boiling water, and takes practice to perfect, so err on the side of caution the first time you make them. The method is slightly scary but as this is the way they have been made for centuries, who am I to complain about hot knuckles?

You can add 2 teaspoons of dried *methi* (fenugreek) to the mix or stud the discs with a few cracked black peppercorns if you like.

Do remember to knead the dough well so that it is supple and does not crack. Also make sure you roll the discs out nice and thinly. Once cooked, the pastries can be kept in an airtight container for up to a week.

MAKES 36

900 g (2 lb) plain white flour

2 teaspoons salt

2 tablespoons carom seeds

rapeseed oil for deep-frying + 1½ cups for preparation

1 Put the flour in a large mixing bowl and add the salt and carom seeds.

2 Heat up 1½ cups of rapeseed oil and add to the flour.

3 Blend together using hands.

4 Add 1 cup of boiling water and gather the mixture together. Add ½ cup more of boiling water.

5 Knead with hands to create a dough that has the texture of Playdoh – not too soft but not too hard as it will crack when rolling. It should be harder than *roti* dough.

6 Divide the mixture evenly into 36 portions. Take a portion and roll into a little ball. Roll out into thin, large-biscuit-like discs. Prick the discs all over with a fork and place on a plate.

7 Heat the oil to about 170°C or when a small piece of the dough rises to the surface at once. Place the discs in the oil and, turning with a perforated spoon, fry until lightly golden – they should not be too dark or too white either.

8 Drain on kitchen paper. Allow to cool and serve on their own.

PANEER MUNCHIES

Okay, I have a small confession to make. I held a dinner party in the summer of 2001 and, as many of my non-Asian friends had never tried *paneer*, I thought I would make these as a starter to introduce them to its charms. The cubes become golden and crispy on the outside, encrusted with the mouth-watering spices, whilst the centre remains pure and silky. The only problem is, they are a bit like Pringles – once you pop you just can't stop! I actually cooked a very large amount and arranged them in a lovely bowl of lollo rosso leaves. I had one, convincing myself that it would not make a difference. About 3 minutes later I had hoovered almost the entire bowl. I felt very ashamed and guilty, like some sort of addict who had spiralled out of control, and stared at the sad looking five cubes left peeking from behind the lettuce. The doorbell rang so I quickly transferred it to a smaller dish, which I presented to my friend Sara, closely followed by Caroline and Louise who, to my dismay, loved them. 'Any more?' they asked. I quickly mumbled 'erm, no, didn't know if you would like them so didn't make many, Bombay mix anyone?' Very, very naughty of me and I do apologise.

SERVES 2 AS A SUBSTANTIAL STARTER

1 teaspoon garam masala

1 teaspoon cumin seeds

1 teaspoon dried red chilli flakes

¼ teaspoon ground turmeric

1 teaspoon dried fenugreek leaves

coarse sea salt

0.305 kg block of paneer (you can use a large block of Greek halloumi cheese instead but then do not add any extra salt), chopped into bite-size pieces

2 tablespoons mild olive oil (not extra virgin)

1 garlic clove, halved lengthways

slices of lime, to garnish

rocket or lollo rosso leaves, to serve

1 In a shallow dish, sprinkle the garam masala, cumin seeds, red chilli flakes, turmeric, dried fenugreek and a good grind of coarse sea salt.

2 Roll the *paneer* cubes in this mixture until they are coated. The moist texture of the *paneer* will ensure the spices stick to it.

3 In a large frying pan, heat the oil and fry the garlic until lightly sizzling. Immediately add the *paneer* and fry until golden. Remove with a slotted spoon and drain on kitchen paper. Discard the oil and garlic.

4 Serve on a bed of lollo rosso or rocket leaves with a twist of lime and Ten-Second Yogurt and Mint Chutney (page 176).

Aloo tikkia

(a-loo-tikk-eea)

FRIED POTATO CAKES

My **Chachiji** made these for me a while ago as an afternoon snack. They are slightly tangy little mashed-potato cakes flavoured with pomegranate-seed powder, coated in gram-flour batter and then deep-fried to create scrummy little snacks. I had tried ready-made versions before but found them uncomfortable to eat due to the high red-chilli-powder content. These milder alternatives are delicious dipped in Ten-Second Yogurt and Mint Chutney (page 176) and bring a little warmth to a rainy afternoon in front of the TV.

MAKES 12

4 potatoes

1 large onion

rapeseed oil for deep-frying + 20 ml (1 tablepoon
   + 1 teaspoon)

1 tablespoon cumin seeds

1 tablespoon salt

1 tablespoon garam masala

2 green chillies, chopped finely

a good handful of chopped fresh coriander

2 teaspoons pomegranate-seed powder

1 cup gram flour

1 Make the filling in exactly the same way as for *samose* (page 49), without the peas and adding the 2 teaspoons of pomegranate-seed powder with the other spices.

2 Take the gram flour and mix with enough cold water to make a slightly runny paste.

3 Divide the potato mixture into 12 equal portions. Take a portion and roll into a ball and then flatten to make an even disc. Repeat with the remaining portions and place on a plate. Wash hands.

4 Heat the oil to around 170°C or when a drop of the mixture rises to the surface at once.

5 Dip each disc into the gram-flour paste to coat well and place in the oil. Fry in batches of six at a time until golden brown.

6 Drain on kitchen paper.

Pakore

(pahk-or-re)

GRAM FLOUR VEGETABLE FRITTERS

When I was very young, I always imagined that these would be quite complicated to make, but they couldn't be simpler. They are perfect for when unexpected guests turn up and you have nothing but a couple of potatoes and an onion lying around. These little handfuls of potato and onion pieces caught in a web of lightly spiced batter are crispy on the outside and succulent and juicy on the inside. They are usually served at teatime with ketchup or *imli* chutney and Indian cardamom tea. They are also so versatile that you can make them with almost any ingredient – chopped vegetables such as cauliflower or aubergine, small pieces of fish or even cubes of *paneer*. They are without a doubt a minimum-effort, maximum-taste snack.

MAKES ABOUT 10

1 cup gram flour

rapeseed oil for deep-frying + 1 tablespoon

1 teaspoon salt

1 teaspoon garam masala

2 green chillies, chopped finely

a good handful of chopped fresh fenugreek
  leaves

1 potato, peeled, cut into thick chips and then
  sliced widthways

½ large onion, halved again lengthways and
  then sliced thinly widthways

1 Take the gram flour (you can sift it first if it makes it easier for you) and place in a large mixing bowl. Add 1 tablespoon of hot rapeseed oil that has been heated in a small pan. Add the salt, garam masala, chillies and fenugreek leaves.

2 Put the oil on to heat ready for deep-frying.

3 Combine this flour mixture with water, using your hands, to make a slightly runny mixture. Not too runny though, it should still be able to hold all the ingredients together. Add the potato and onion and mix with your hands.

4 The oil should be at about 170°C. Drop a tiny bit of the batter into the oil. If it rises to the surface immediately, then the oil is hot enough. Take little handfuls of the mixture and, with fingers, drop them into the oil. If this is too scary, use a perforated spoon. Make sure they are dropped very close to the surface of the oil so it doesn't splash. Keep turning with a perforated spoon and fry until golden brown.

5 Remove with a clean slotted spoon and drain on kitchen paper. Serve with ketchup or chutneys.

Gurudwara

The Gurudwara is the Sikh Temple,

a place chosen by Sikhs for meeting and speaking about God,

for public worship and for religious ceremonies.

These buildings are usually very simple inside.

They have a kitchen in which to prepare the Langar

(the meal provided at the Gurudwara), an area to place shoes

and wash hands and the main prayer room.

This room is divided into two seating areas

by a pathway along the centre of the floor.

The men sit on the floor on one side and the women on the other.

The path leads to the focal point at the front of the room

where the Guru Granth Sahib (see opposite)

is placed on a platform under a canopy.

The Gurudwara is recognised by a tall flag pole

draped in yellow cloth with a yellow flag

clearly showing the symbol of the Khanda.

This is the holy symbol comprising a quoit

with a dagger at the centre and two curved swords

with the handles crossing underneath.

Heads must be covered and shoes removed

before entering a Gurudwara.

The prayer room at the *Gurudwara* (temple)

VICKY'S AMAZING POTATOES

I made this dish up in my early teens when I was bored of eating regular jacket potatoes. The original recipe comes from – and I cannot believe I am actually admitting this – a Rainbow annual my Mum bought for me one Christmas when I was little (yes, that's right, of the Bungle, Zippy and George variety). I was intrigued by a recipe of theirs that involved scooping out the potato, mashing it with butter and cheese and then placing the mixture back into the jacket shell to brown under the grill. I decided to add some bright vegetables, chilli and lemon juice to make these into an exciting snack. See, jacket potatoes don't have to be boring!

SERVES 4

4 large baking potatoes

250 g (9 oz) cheese (I use red Leicester, as I
  love the colour and nutty taste)

a knob of butter

2 spring onions, chopped finely

2 tomatoes, diced

1 pepper of any colour, de-seeded and diced (I
  like using yellow)

¼ cucumber, diced

coarse sea salt

coarsely ground black pepper

a generous dash of lemon juice

1 teaspoon red chilli powder

¼ teaspoon garam masala

1 pickled chilli, chopped finely

a handful of chopped fresh coriander

1 Preheat the oven to 200°C/fan oven 180°C/Gas Mark 6. Prick the potatoes with a fork, wash and microwave until almost done (so the flesh is soft but not too mushy).

2 In the meantime, grate the cheese into a large mixing bowl and add the remaining ingredients.

3 Take the potatoes out of the microwave and slice off the tops. Scoop out the potato flesh and add to the mixing bowl with the other ingredients. Mix well using a fork.

4 Place the potato tops (skin-side down) and shells on a piece of foil on a baking sheet.

5 Spoon the mixture into the shells and on to the tops, piling it high.

6 Bake for about 15 minutes until the mixture is browned and bubbling. Serve immediately, with lots of salad leaves.

Guru Granth Sahib

Sikhs do not worship any idols
but instead have a sacred book containing the teachings
of the ten Gurus. All Sikhs revere this holy book.

The Marriage Ceremony

Whilst the couple are seated before the Guru Granth Sahib,
prayers are read. They then stand and the bride holds one end of a sash
whilst the other is held by the bridegroom. Holding this sash, the groom
leads the bride in a circuit around the Guru Granth Sahib.
Once this has been repeated four times, they bow in acceptance and
listen to the religious obligations of married life.

Andda bread

(an-dhaa)

FRIED EGGY BREAD

The 1970s: a riot of a time for anyone and for British Asians the decade smacks of long sideburns, swirly patterned multicolour wallpaper, Indian suits with flary bottoms and mini tunics and plaits which were coiled up to form two big loops at either side of the head, fastened with bright chunky plastic bobbles. It was a time when youngsters hid behind the trees whilst eating their *parathe* during a family picnic at the park or ate them in the car on their way to relatives in *Kwentry, Bul-bulhampton* or *Slo* (Coventry, Wolverhampton and Slough to the rest of us) and longed for fish fingers. This is one of those snacks created at that time and is inspired by the great British fry-up. It is delicious, cheap and filling and was the perfect treat for kids whilst they watched The Magic Roundabout (which, incidentally, my Mum watched on her black and white TV holding sweet wrappers in front of her eyes to make it colour – the 70s eh?)!

MAKES 3 SLICES (A SNACK FOR 1 PERSON)

1 egg

½ cup milk

3 slices of white bread, crusts cut off

oil, for deep-frying

For a sweet version:

3 teaspoons sugar

For a savoury version:

½ teaspoon salt

1 teaspoon garam masala

1 finely chopped green chilli (optional)

1 Beat the egg with the milk using a fork, until frothy. Add the sugar (for a sweet eggy bread) or the salt, garam masala and chilli (for a savoury version) and beat a little more.

2 Soak the bread in the mixture for a couple of seconds, turning over until each side is well coated.

3 Heat the oil to 170°C or until a drop of the egg mixture rises at once.

4 Using a fish slice, drop the bread into the oil to deep-fry until golden and crisp.

5 Eat with a sprinkling of more sugar or ketchup.

POOIJI'S ORIGINAL FRITTERS

My Pooiji recently introduced me to these truly spectacular fritters. Pooiji really is quite legendary indeed when it comes to her food. She is one of those people who has an unlimited enthusiasm for life and is on a constant quest to learn as many new things as possible, to better herself and then pass on all this knowledge to those around her. She is famed for her home-making skills and her sewing but most of all, her cooking. She treats it as an art form and takes great care with the tastes, giving full attention to each tiny little detail. The crunchy exterior of these lentil fritters gives way upon biting to a moist centre crammed with potato, onion, chilli and plump raisins. An unusual combination, but unforgettable. Served with Chutney For Guests (page 177), these make an impressive treat.

MAKES ABOUT 10

1 cup mahaar dhal 2-pieces (split urid beans)	**1 small onion, chopped finely**
1 teaspoon cumin seeds	**a handful of chopped fresh coriander**
1½ teaspoons salt	**¼ cup raisins**
1 teaspoon grated fresh ginger (do not use frozen as it's difficult to blend)	**4 green chillies chopped finely**
	1 potato, peeled and chopped finely
4 tablespoons gram flour	

1   Soak the dhal in a pan of water overnight.

2   The next day, rub the dhal well in the water to remove the skins. Rinse the dhal well several times with water. The pressure of the water coming from the tap into the pan will lift the skins to the surface. Repeat this process until almost all of the skins have been removed and you are left with the dhal.

3   Drain the dhal and place in a blender. Blend until very smooth.

4   Add the cumin seeds, salt, ginger, gram flour, onion, coriander, raisins, chillies and potato and mix well with a fork.

5   Divide the mixture evenly into little balls. Flatten into patties.

6   Heat the oil to 170°C or until a drop of the mixture rises to the surface at once. Place the fritters in the oil and fry until golden.

7   Drain on kitchen paper and serve with Chutney For Guests (page 177).

Tarke andde

(thur-khe-an-dhe)

VERY SPECIAL EGGS

I think just about every British-Asian household loves these delicious scrambled eggs. Asian people find bland food very hard to swallow and so have added their own touch to transform simple eggs into this explosion of taste and colour. They are so easy and quick to make that this is the perfect dish for when you haven't done the shopping or have no energy to cook full-on Indian food but still want the taste. The perfect dish for hungry people who want food now, this is good for students who want to impress when they feel like coming over all *desi*. Delicious with toast and ketchup or *roti* and lime *achaar*, these can be eaten at any time. My sister hates eggs but really loves these, that's how good they are.

SERVES 2

3 eggs

½ teaspoon salt

1 teaspoon garam masala

1 green chilli, chopped finely

2 spring onions, chopped finely

a handful of chopped fresh coriander

1 tomato, chopped finely

¼ red pepper, de-seeded and chopped finely

¼ onion, chopped finely

1 garlic clove, chopped finely

a dash of lemon juice

¼ teaspoon ground turmeric

a good knob of butter

1 Break the eggs into a mixing bowl and beat well with a fork.

2 Add all the remaining ingredients except the butter and beat well with the fork.

3 Gently heat the butter in a large frying pan.

4 Add the egg mixture and stir continuously with a wooden spoon until the eggs are soft and fluffy.

DRY MASALA MIXED NUTS

I am a big fan of all sorts of nuts, especially brazil nuts, but am usually limited to plain, pre-packed salted or dry roasted. This recipe is are unusual in that the nuts are served hot and sizzling straight from the pan, coated in deep, earthy, smoky spices and then topped with a smattering of juicy coriander leaf. They make decadent pre-dinner nibbles to serve with drinks and impart a delicious aroma around the house.

SERVES 4 AS NIBBLES WITH DRINKS

¼ cup mild olive oil

1 teaspoon cumin seeds

1 teaspoon garam masala

2 cloves

1 teaspoon salt

½ teaspoon pomegranate-seed powder

¼ teaspoon red chilli powder

a small piece of cassia bark

2½ cups unsalted, shelled mixed nuts

a handful of chopped fresh coriander (do not use frozen as it will make the nuts soggy)

1 Place the oil in a large frying pan and add the cumin seeds. Fry gently on a very low heat for a few seconds.

2 Add the remaining spices and fry very gently for 2 minutes, stirring with a wooden spatula.

3 Add the nuts, coat well and continue to fry for 5 minutes.

4 Pour into a serving dish, garnish with chopped fresh coriander and serve immediately.

Me being taught how to make *Jalebia* (sweet batter coils) by a street vendor

sabjia

(sahb-ji-aah)

VEGETARIAN DISHES

Sukke chole

(suk-he-sho-le)

DRY CHICK-PEAS

The majority of my non-Asian friends have only eaten chick-peas either in a cold salad or ground into hummus. That is a shame as cooked chick-peas make a delicious and nutritious meal. A couple of cans in the pantry are all you really need to create this full-flavoured dish. The recipe here is for the dry version, which has only a little densely flavoured sauce to coat the buttery chick-peas, and is then topped with crunchy spring onions. It is usually served with *samose* and *palhe* at parties but is also fantastic with *bhature* and *bhoondiwala dahi* (pages 169 and 180). If you would like to make the version with a more liquid sauce, simply add enough water at step 4 to cover the chick-peas, cover and simmer for 20 minutes.

SERVES 4 — 6

2 tablespoons oil	½ teaspoon ground turmeric
½ large onion, sliced thinly	1 teaspoon garam masala
2 garlic cloves, chopped finely	1½ teaspoons salt
½ cup canned chopped tomatoes, whizzed in a blender	a dash of lime juice
	a handful of chopped fresh coriander
1 green chilli, chopped finely	2 x 400 g cans of chick-peas, drained
1 teaspoon grated fresh root ginger	2 spring onions, chopped finely, to garnish

1 Heat the oil and add the onion and garlic. Fry until golden brown.

2 Turn down the heat and add the tomatoes, chilli, ginger, turmeric, garam masala, salt, lime juice and a good handful of coriander. Stir well and add a splash of water. When shiny and the oil separates, add the chick-peas.

3 Turn up the heat and stir-fry for a few minutes.

4 Add ½ cup of water, turn the heat down, cover and simmer for 15 minutes, stirring halfway through.

5 Turn off the heat and garnish with the spring onions.

Mattar paneer

(mah-tar-pa-neer)

PEAS AND CREAM CHEESE

This is a real classic heart-warming Punjabi dish. It has a velvety, even, balanced sauce, which gently envelops the smooth *paneer* and the bouncy peas. As *paneer* is so rich, it is better not to fry it before adding, as some people do, as this just adds to the cholesterol level. If you add the *paneer* straight to the pan, it stays soft and supple.

Some people find it slightly difficult to digest *paneer* so I have included *Pooiji's* solution. Drawing on age-old Indian herbalist knowledge, she boils cardamom, cassia bark and bay leaves in water, which creates an elixir that she then adds to the sauce. It does not impart any flavour; its purpose is purely to ensure that the stomach remains balanced. *Paneer* can also sometimes erm … exacerbate wind, but for that one, she says you're on your own! Make sure that you cut the *paneer* in dice proportional to the size of the peas – large, uneven pieces of anything rarely look presentable and neat. Serve with simple *roti* and a carrot *achaar* (page 187)

SERVES 4 – 6

¾ cup oil

1 teaspoon cumin seeds

2 cloves

1 large onion, chopped roughly

3 garlic cloves, chopped

4 canned whole plum tomatoes and a dash of
  the juice, whizzed in a blender

3 green chillies, chopped finely

2 teaspoons grated fresh root ginger

2 teaspoons salt

2 teaspoons garam masala

2 teaspoons ground turmeric

3 cups frozen peas

0.305 kg block of paneer, diced

½ teaspoon white sugar

4 green cardamom pods

2 brown cardamom pods

1 cassia stick

2 bay leaves

½ teaspoon tandoori masala powder

a handful of chopped fresh coriander

1 Heat the oil in a large pan with the cumin seeds and the cloves.

2 When the cumin has begun to sizzle, add the onion and garlic. Turn the heat down to low, cover with a lid and cook very gently for 10 minutes. This is so that the onions sweat and the ingredients release all their flavour without the onion frying or turning golden. The onion should be soft and translucent.

3 Turn off the heat and, using a slotted spoon, place the onion mixture in a blender, leaving the oil behind in the pan. Blend until smooth.

4 Place the pan with the oil back on a medium heat and when it has reheated, return the onion mixture to the pan. Stir well with a wooden spoon.

5 When the onions are a lovely golden brown, lower the heat, wait for about 1 minute and add the tomato and chillies (this is so it doesn't spit).

6 Turn the heat up slightly and add the ginger. Stir for 5 minutes until the mixture is shiny and the oil separates.

7 Add the salt, garam masala and turmeric. Stir well and then turn down the heat a little.

8 Add the peas and stir well to coat. Turn back up to a medium heat and cover for 5 minutes.

9 Add the *paneer* cubes and 3 cups of boiling water. Stir well. Add the sugar. Cover and leave to simmer for 30 minutes.

10 Roughly smash the green and brown cardamom and the cassia bark in a pestle and mortar.

11 Place 1 cup of water in a small saucepan, add the spices from the pestle and mortar and bay leaves and bring to the boil. Leave boiling for 10 minutes. Strain the water into the pan with the *paneer* and peas.

12 Add the tandoori masala and stir. Sprinkle with a handful of coriander before serving.

CHEAT'S SAAG

I was at my Chachiji's house a while ago and, whilst talking about food, I mentioned that I hadn't eaten saag in a very long time (because it takes so long to make – wait till you read the recipe, this will seem a doddle). She explained that there is a way to make a quick version of saag, which, although not the same as real traditional saag (page 193), is a very tasty, quick alternative. She then set about making some for me and I protested, feeling very guilty as she had already made some dishes and I certainly didn't want her to go to the extra trouble. But that is the thing in my family; everyone always shares their very best food with me, which is very kind of them indeed. The result was a delicious saag for whenever you crave it, and cannot wait 2 hours, and is perfect with parathe, plain dahi, lemon achaar and a dollop of butter.

SERVES 4 – 6

794 g can of puréed *palak* (spinach)

4 green chillies, chopped finely

½ teaspoon salt

½ cup coarse corn flour

½ cup oil

1 onion, sliced thinly

4 garlic cloves, chopped finely

3 canned whole plum tomatoes, whizzed in
 a blender

1 teaspoon grated fresh root ginger

butter, to serve

1 Pour the canned *palak* into a saucepan and add 1 cup of water. Stir well and bring to the boil. Simmer for 15 minutes.

2 Add the chillies and salt. Using a hand-mixer, mix the *palak* right there in the pan for 2 minutes.

3 When excess water has evaporated, leave to cook gently for 10 minutes.

4 Add the corn flour and 1 cup of boiling water and use the hand-mixer again to blend until of a smooth, thick and even consistency. Switch off the heat.

5 In a frying pan, heat the oil and add the onion and garlic. Fry to a deep golden brown. Lower the heat and wait for 1 minute before adding the tomatoes and ginger. Continue to fry for 5 more minutes and then add to the *palak* mixture. Stir well.

6 Top with a good knob of butter.

Tinde

(teen-de)

INDIAN BABY PUMPKINS

This is a real Punjabi treasure. Pale green, bursting with sweetness, nestled with tender potatoes and steamed in a light whisper of a sauce, these baby pumpkins are a delight. They are only available from Indian grocers but, if you have an Indian community a short car ride away, it is worth making the journey to hunt them down. If this is not possible then you can use baby turnips instead, adding a little more sugar at the end of cooking to suit. As this is such a simple and pure dish it really needs no other accompaniment than roti and a touch of plain dahi. Anything else will swamp the delicate wash of flavours.

SERVES 4 — 6

2 tablespoons butter

1 onion, chopped finely

1 garlic clove, chopped finely

¼ teaspoon ground turmeric

¼ cup chopped canned tomatoes, whizzed in the blender

1 green chilli, chopped finely

1 teaspoon grated fresh root ginger

1 teaspoon garam masala

1½ teaspoons salt

2 handfuls of chopped fresh coriander

½ teaspoon white sugar

4 tinde, topped and tailed with the skin scraped off with a knife, cut into small chunks

3 potatoes, peeled and cut into chunks the same size as the tinde

butter, to serve

1 Heat the 2 tablespoons of butter in a saucepan and, when melted, add the onion and garlic and fry until very lightly golden. (Most people use this frying time to prepare the vegetables).

2 Lower the heat and add the turmeric, tomatoes, chilli and ginger. Add a splash of water to prevent the mixture becoming too dry. Stir well and add the garam masala, salt, a good handful of coriander and the sugar. Stir well.

3 Once the mixture has become shiny and the oil has begun to separate (add splashes of water if necessary), add the vegetables and stir well to coat thoroughly with the mixture.

4 Turn up the heat and stir-fry for about 5 minutes.

5 Add ¼ cup boiling water, reduce to a low heat, cover and cook gently for 15–20 minutes until the potatoes are soft. Carefully stir occasionally to check it is not sticking to the bottom.

6 Turn the heat off and serve with a knob of butter and a sprinkling of more chopped coriander.

Kale chole

(kaa-le-sho-le)
BLACK CHICK-PEAS

Whilst regular chick-peas are plump, easy to squish with your fingers and a pale sunshine colour, these are the smaller, dried variations which are firmer and turn darker, hence the name of this dish, and are distinctly earthy and nutty. As their flavour is so woodily deep, they need to be supported by a richer masala than most vegetarian dishes. Therefore, this sauce is similar to that used for meat dishes, with lots of browned onion, tomato and rich garam *masala* to blanket these smoky little nuggets. Serve with *roti*, a light vegetable dish such as *gajar, aloo, mattar* (page 86) and plain *dahi*.

SERVES 4

½ cup dried chick-peas with skins

⅓ cup oil

1 teaspoon cumin seeds

2 cloves

1 onion, chopped roughly

2 garlic cloves, chopped roughly

½ cup canned chopped tomatoes, whizzed in
   a blender

1 green chilli, chopped finely

1 teaspoon grated fresh root ginger

1½ teaspoons salt

1½ teaspoons garam masala

1 teaspoon ground turmeric

a handful of chopped fresh coriander

1   Wash the chick-peas and leave to soak in a pan of water with a pinch of salt overnight.

2   The next day, using the same water the chick-peas were soaking in, put the pan on to a medium heat. Bring to the boil and simmer for 30 minutes.

3   Heat the oil in a saucepan with the cumin seeds and the cloves. When sizzling, add the onion and garlic. Cover and cook on a very low heat for 10 minutes. Turn off the heat. Using a slotted spoon, transfer the onion to a blender and whizz till smooth, leaving the oil in the pan.

4   Put the pan with the oil back on the heat and when hot, add the blended onion. Fry until golden brown. Turn the heat down and add the tomatoes, chilli, ginger, salt, garam masala and turmeric. Add a splash of water and cook gently, stirring, until the oil has separated and the mixture is shiny.

5   Using a slotted spoon, add the chick-peas and stir-fry for a few minutes. Add the water they have been simmering in. Bring to the boil, cover and simmer for 25 minutes.

6   Stir well and raise the heat for a couple of minutes so the sauce thickens slightly. Sprinkle with a handful of chopped coriander before serving.

Aloo methi

(a-loo-me-thee)

POTATOES WITH FENUGREEK LEAF

I have tried to make this dish with dried methi but found the result was not quite the same, as dried fenugreek leaves are overpoweringly pungent and have the texture of lawnmower cuttings. Dried fenugreek is great when used sparingly to add a little kick to snacks but for this dish, where the fenugreek is performing in a starring role, there is no substitute for the real thing. Bunches of fresh methi leaves can be found at all Indian grocery stores and it is best to buy a few bunches, chop finely and then freeze in large bags which will keep for a good few months. Added to simple potatoes, these green leaves transform the taste and create a fragrant dish screaming with flavour. Eat as an accompaniment to a meat dish or simply with rice or roti.

SERVES 2 — 4

2 tablespoons oil

¼ teaspoon cumin seeds

¼ teaspoon fenugreek seeds

½ onion, chopped finely

1 garlic clove, chopped finely

½ cup canned chopped tomatoes, whizzed in
a blender

1 teaspoon ground turmeric

1½ teaspoons garam masala

1½ teaspoons salt

2 green chillies, chopped finely

1 teaspoon grated fresh root ginger

3 potatoes, peeled and cubed

1 bunch of fresh fenugreek, chopped finely

butter, to serve

1   Heat the oil in a saucepan with the cumin and fenugreek seeds. When gently sizzling, add the onion and garlic. Gently fry, stirring all the time, until lightly golden.

2   Turn the heat down and add the tomatoes. Stir well. Add the turmeric, garam masala, salt, chillies and ginger. Stir well. Cook gently until the mixture has become shiny and the oil separates. Add splashes of water if necessary. Leave to cook for a further minute.

3   Add the potatoes. Stir well to coat and stir-fry for 5 minutes. Add the fenugreek and stir well to mix all the ingredients together.

4   Add 1 cup of boiling water and stir for 1 minute. Raise the heat and bring to the boil. Reduce the heat, cover and leave to simmer for 15–20 minutes until the potatoes are tender. Check the mixture halfway through this time to check it is not sticking to the bottom of the pan. Add a splash more water if necessary.

5   Turn off the heat and top with a knob of butter.

Karele parkhe

(kah-rel-e-parr-khe)

STUFFED BITTER GOURD

I was very young when I saw my Mum making these for the first time. I sat horrified in the living room, watching her in the kitchen through the open door as she cooked what I thought at that time were rats, dropping them into hot oil by the tail. The shape of the gourd, with its dark knobbly exterior and long thin tail does, in fairness, look like a rodent from a distance…well, when you're five years old it does. Much later, having reached the conclusion that my Mum was not in fact into ritual rat-cooking, I tasted this speciality. It is an acquired taste but after you have tried it a few times it becomes a treat for the taste buds. I suppose it is like when people try alcohol for the first time and spit it out, only later appreciating the complex flavour notes. These are flavoured with pomegranate and chilli and then baked with tomato and coriander to make an amazing side dish. *Karele* are also very good for cleansing the blood – all the more reason to enjoy!

SERVES 6

6 karele

salt, for rubbing

oil, for deep-frying

very finely chopped de-seeded tomato

a handful of chopped fresh coriander

For the filling:

4 tablespoons oil

2 onions, ground in a blender

1 teaspoon salt

¼ teaspoon ground turmeric

2 green chillies, chopped finely

½ teaspoon pomegranate-seed powder

½ teaspoon sugar

1 teaspoon garam masala

1 Using a small sharp knife, scrape off the knobbly bits of the skin. To stop *karele* knobbles flying all over the kitchen, do this by holding the *karela* in one hand, the knife with the blade horizontal in the other and literally slice them off. Once the knobbles are off, scrape the blade over the surface to leave the *karele* smooth and bright green.

2 Cut a slit along the length of each *karela*, making sure not to go through to the ends or through to the other side. Gently open the *karela* and, using a teaspoon, scoop out the large seeds inside.

3 Rub lots of salt inside and outside the *karele*. Leave to sit while you make the filling.

4 Heat the oil in a large frying pan and, when hot, add the onions. Fry on a low heat. When you can no longer smell the strong smell of the onion and it is a tiny bit golden, add the salt, turmeric, chillies, pomegranate-seed powder, sugar and garam masala. Stir well and fry gently for a few minutes. Turn the heat off and leave to cool.

5 Rinse the *karele* of the salt, squeeze any excess water out and drain on kitchen paper.

6 Heat the oil in the deep fryer to about 170°C or when a small bit of the filling rises to the surface at once. Deep-fry the *karele* until they are golden brown. Remove and drain on kitchen paper.

7 Using a teaspoon, fully stuff the *karele* with the onion mixture. Place in a baking dish and sprinkle with the tomato and a handful of chopped coriander. Bake in an oven preheated to 220°C/fan oven 180°C/Gas Mark 6 for 25 minutes.

8 Alternatively, you can bind them with string or use toothpicks soaked in water to hold the stuffing in and shallow-fry them for 10 minutes.

Shimla mirch parkhe

(shim-laa-mirch-parr-khe)

STUFFED PEPPERS

I absolutely cannot do this dish justice with mere words. This is, without a shadow of a doubt, one of the most delicious things I have ever eaten in my life. Whole juicy peppers in a gem-like array of colours, blistered on the outside to give a smoky charred-ness, oozing with moisture inside, filled with a piquant, silky mash of potato, onion, dried red chilli and ginger. The tartness of the filling contrasts perfectly with the blushing sweetness of the peppers. They appeal to all five senses, from the crackling sound as they emerge from the oven to the visual feast for the eye as they are piled into an earthenware dish as the table centrepiece. I ate these with *thomi mahaar dhal* (page 94), *roti*, plain *dahi* and lemon *achaar* and it was a meal I will never forget.

SERVES 6

6 large peppers of different colours

oil, for drizzling

For the filling:

4 potatoes, peeled and chopped into small chunks

½ cup oil

1 teaspoon cumin seeds

2 onions, chopped very finely

1½ teaspoons dried red chilli flakes

1 teaspoon grated fresh root ginger

2 teaspoons salt

1 teaspoon garam masala

1 teaspoon pomegranate-seed powder

a good handful of chopped fresh coriander

1 Preheat the oven to 200°C/fan oven 180°C/Gas Mark 6. Boil the potatoes until soft; drain.

2 Heat the oil in a large frying pan with the cumin seeds. When sizzling, fry the onions until soft but not golden. Add the chilli, ginger, salt, garam masala, pomegranate-seed powder and potatoes. Turn off the heat and mash the mixture together in the pan. Add the coriander and mash a little more.

3 Cut out the stalks of the peppers by gently using a knife to cut around it and then pull them out. They should look like plugs or stoppers and you should be left with the whole pepper with a hole at the top. Do not discard the stalks.

4 Stuff the peppers with the potato mixture, using fingers to press in as much as you can. When the peppers are full, push the stalks back in. Push them quite far into the pepper as during cooking they will be pushed out slightly; they should give the impression of a whole pepper again. Place on a baking tray and drizzle with a little oil.

5 Bake in the preheated oven for 45 minutes, turning over halfway.

Andde di sabji

(an·dhe·dee·sahb·jee)

BOILED EGGS IN SAUCE

You come home one night to find you only have a few eggs in the fridge and the odd potato or two – doesn't sound very appetising does it? Well, here is a satisfying dish loaded with the delicious flavours of tandoori masala, ginger and garlic and carrying the aroma of bay leaf, cassia bark and cloves. The sauce, which should not be watery but definitely liquid, is perfect for the potatoes and soft eggs with their creamy, crumbly golden yolks. My Dad used to make this a lot when I was young and I would watch as the humble and inexpensive ingredients were transformed to key players in a masterpiece dish. Serve with rice or roti.

SERVES 4 – 6

4 eggs

½ cup oil

1 teaspoon cumin seeds

1 cassia stick

2 cloves

1 bay leaf

1 onion, very finely chopped

2 garlic cloves, very finely chopped

½ cup canned chopped tomatoes, whizzed in
　　a blender

2 green chillies, chopped finely

2 handfuls of chopped fresh coriander

2 teaspoons grated fresh root ginger

2 teaspoons salt

1 teaspoon garam masala

2 teaspoons turmeric

1 teaspoon tandoori masala powder

¼ teaspoon sugar

6 small potatoes, peeled and quartered

1 Hard-boil the eggs in a pan of boiling water with a drop of vinegar for about 8 minutes. Rinse in lots of cold running water to stop the eggs cooking and then leave to cool completely.

2 Heat the oil in a large saucepan with the cumin seeds, cassia bark, cloves and bay leaf. When sizzling, add the onion and garlic. Turn the heat down very low and gently sweat the onions for 5 minutes, stirring all the time. Cover and leave to cook gently for another 5 minutes. Remove the cloves, cassia bark and bay leaf. Turn up the heat and fry until golden, pressing the onions against the side of the pan with a wooden spoon to crush.

3 Turn the heat down and add the tomatoes, chillies, a good handful of chopped coriander, ginger, salt, garam masala, turmeric and tandoori masala. Add a splash of water and cook until shiny and the oil separates. Add the sugar. Stir well.

4 Add the potatoes and stir well to coat thoroughly. Add 3 cups of boiling water, bring to the boil and then cover and leave to simmer for 20 minutes or until the potatoes are soft.

5 Shell the eggs and cut them in half lengthways with a very sharp knife. Place them on top of the potatoes in the pan, with the yolks facing upwards. Spoon over some of the sauce. Replace the lid and cook on a very low heat for a further 10 minutes. Turn off the heat and sprinkle with more chopped coriander.

OVEN-BAKED CHERRY TOMATOES WITH SAFFRON

This is a dish I created after buying a wonderfully rustic-looking pack of scarlet baby tomatoes still attached to the vine. They looked as though they deserved the most exquisite flavours. These tomatoes are cooked gently with sugar, cardamom and saffron, creating a hedonistic veil until the tomatoes burst through it willing to yield all their sweetness. This seasoning combines Mediterranean and regal Indian flavours and the tomatoes are lovely tossed with pasta and a little goat's cheese, used as a jacket potato topping, with *parathe* or as a side dish to Green Masala Roast Chicken (page 109).

SERVES 2 – 4

375 g pack of cherry tomatoes	**a sprinkle of white sugar**
mild olive oil	**a sprinkle of salt**
2 cloves	**4 drops of light malt vinegar**
2 green cardamoms	**a few saffron strands**
a sprinkle of garam masala	

1 Preheat the oven to 200°C/fan oven 180°C/Gas Mark 6. Place the tomatoes evenly in a baking dish.

2 Drizzle with the olive oil.

3 Push the cloves and cardamom between the tomatoes and sprinkle the rest of the ingredients over the top.

4 Bake in the hot oven until the tomatoes are soft and blistered.

PASTA WITH YOGURT AND CHILLI DRIZZLE

I eat this all the time, at least once a week. My friend and old flatmate, Lara, introduced me to this a while ago having been shown the dish by her Turkish friend's mother. When she initially described the dish I thought it sounded awful – cold yogurt on hot pasta topped with hot oil. 'Er, no thanks, mate', was my initial response but she quite rightly convinced me that it was a delicious combination of flavours, textures and temperatures. I watched avidly as she heated the oil with harissa powder and then poured it, sizzling, over the yogurt-coated pasta. I have created my own variation with dried chilli flakes and red onion. This is wonderful comfort food and is also very healthy.

SERVES 1

pasta of your choice and in the amount you
  desire (I like to use tri-colour spirals)

olive oil

a few very thin slices of red onion

1 garlic clove, chopped finely

¼ teaspoon dried red chilli flakes

¼ teaspoon cumin seeds

salt and pepper

small tub of low-fat natural yogurt (not set),
  to serve

1 Place the pasta in a saucepan of boiling, salty water to cook according to the packet instructions.

2 Meanwhile, pour a good glug of olive oil into a frying pan and add the onions, garlic, chilli, cumin seeds and salt and pepper. On a low heat, gently sizzle the onions, stirring occasionally.

3 Drain the pasta, toss with a little olive oil and pour into a shallow dish, bowl or plate.

4 Top with the yogurt.

5 Turn off the heat and drizzle the oil with the onions over the yogurt on the pasta. Eat immediately.

FINGERLICKING POTATO WEDGES

Potato wedges go down a treat with nearly everyone. I first created these when I was about thirteen and was experimenting in the kitchen whilst half-watching The Fresh Prince of Bel Air. These wedges are made with chilli, black pepper and dried mango powder, which make them fiery and tangy, and are fantastic with Devilish Butter Chicken (page 107) and Ten-second Yogurt and Mint Chutney (page 176) or a little crème fraîche.

SERVES 4

4 potatoes

oil, for drizzling

1 teaspoon salt

¼ teaspoon ground turmeric

¼ teaspoon pomegranate-seed powder

¼ teaspoon red chilli powder

¼ teaspoon dried mango powder

coarsely ground black pepper

a dash of lemon juice

fresh coriander sprigs, to garnish

lemon wedges, to serve

1 Preheat the oven to 200°C/fan oven 180°C/Gas Mark 6. Parboil the potatoes whole with their skins still on. Leave to cool.

2 Using a sharp knife, cut in half lengthways and then at again at angles to create wedges.

3 Place on a baking tray that has been greased with a little oil, skin-side down. Drizzle a little more oil on to the potatoes.

4 Combine the salt, spices and pepper in a bowl and sprinkle over the potatoes. Give the potatoes a good dash of lemon juice and bake till crisp and golden. Garnish with sprigs of coriander and serve with lemon wedges.

HOT BLACK PEPPER BUTTER CUCUMBER

This is a very simple dish. Most people only eat cucumber cold or as a pickle but it takes on a lovely subtle personality when heated through and this recipe allows those qualities to shine through. The richness of the butter accentuates the glassy understated cucumber whilst the pepper adds a little musky depth. Made in a couple of minutes, this is a wonderful accompaniment, especially to tandoori chicken.

SERVES 2

1 tablespoon butter

½ cucumber, diced

salt and pepper

a generous sprinkle of garam masala

a handful of chopped fresh coriander

1 Gently heat the butter in a saucepan and add the cucumber. Stir well. Add a generous grind of salt and pepper and sprinkle in the garam masala. Stir well for a few minutes.
2 Turn off the heat. Sprinkle with the coriander and serve immediately.

MAHARAJAH'S MASH

Mashed spuds are a real British favourite. This mash is thick and buttery but given a slightly sour note with the yogurt and then enriched with the roasted garlic, chilli, red onion, mushrooms and coriander. The result is a very special version of mash, which is delicious with lamb chops, kebabs or any dry chicken. You can add a little grated Cheddar or top with crunchy *sev* (noodles similar to Bombay mix) and *imli* chutney for a quick *chaat* (an Indian snack speciality). This is mash fit for a king, or should I say Maharajah?

SERVES 2

mashed potato for 2 people

1 tablespoon natural set low-fat yogurt

1 tablespoon butter

1 garlic clove, roasted in the oven in its skin
    until melting and then squeezed out

½ teaspoon salt

½ teaspoon garam masala

1 teaspoon dried red chilli flakes

¼ red onion, chopped very finely

4 mushrooms, chopped very finely

a handful of chopped fresh coriander

Stir all the ingredients into the hot mashed potato and mix well.

Gajar, aloo, mattar

(gah-jar, a-loo, mah-tar)

CARROTS, POTATOES AND PEAS

When I was fourteen I spent a week with my cousins Nina Bhenji and Papa Paaji who were both studying in London at the time and had their own house in Hayes. I listened attentively as they both told me about student life. The bit I remember most was the part about how poor I was going to be. They advised me to learn to cook Indian food, as once you know how, you can cook a feast with very little money because the ingredients needed are so very cheap. We sat down that evening to a delicious meal and while students next door ate reheated pizza, again, we ate food as good as that at home. This is what we ate, along with some Quorn mince, roti, dahi and achaar. Simple, rustic and delicious.

SERVES 4 — 6

1 tablespoon oil	1½ teaspoons salt
1 onion, chopped finely	1 teaspoon garam masala
1 garlic clove, chopped finely	1 teaspoon ground turmeric
¼ cup canned chopped tomatoes	6 carrots, sliced
2 green chillies, chopped finely	3 potatoes, peeled and diced
1 teaspoon grated fresh root ginger	2 cups of frozen peas
a handful of chopped fresh coriander	butter, to serve

1 Heat the oil in a pan and add the onion and garlic. Fry until very lightly golden.
2 Add the tomatoes, chillies, ginger, coriander, salt, garam masala and turmeric. Add a good splash of water and cook until the mixture becomes shiny and the oil separates.
3 Add the vegetables and stir well to coat thoroughly with the mixture.
4 Add ¼ cup of water and cover. Cook on a gentle heat for 20 minutes.
5 Turn up the heat to evaporate any remaining water and switch off the heat.
6 Top with a knob of butter.

MANGE TOUT AND BABY CORN

Along with staying true to traditional ingredients, I am always on the look out for new ones. Mange tout and baby corn are wonderful, youthful vegetables that are full of goodness and need very little cooking time. This recipe is all about simply accentuating the flavours with a little mustard seed, stir-frying and then lightly steaming the vegetables through. The result is a modern, contemporary vegetarian dish to enjoy with *pooria* and *palhe*.

SERVES 4

1 tablespoon oil

¼ teaspoon mustard seeds

½ onion, sliced thinly

1 garlic clove, chopped finely

2 fresh tomatoes, diced

1 teaspoon garam masala

1 teaspoon salt

1 teaspoon ground turmeric

1 teaspoon grated fresh root ginger

a squeeze of lime juice

1 packet of fresh mange tout

1 packet of fresh baby corn

a handful of chopped fresh coriander

1 Heat the oil and add the mustard seeds. When they begin to pop, add the onion and garlic. Fry until lightly golden.

2 Add the tomatoes, garam masala, salt, turmeric, ginger, and lime juice. Cook gently until the mixture becomes shiny and the oil separates.

3 Add the vegetables and stir-fry for 5 minutes.

4 Cover and simmer on a very low heat for a further 10 minutes.

5 Before serving, sprinkle with a handful of chopped coriander.

BAKED BEANS WITH SPRING ONION SABJI

When Indians came to this country they eagerly anticipated the culinary delights that would greet them. This was the most loved of them all, good old baked beans. Indians quickly realised their versatility, they were cheap and filling and you could keep cans in the cupboard without them going off. So this is the British-Asian remix version of baked beans, given a little kick of garam masala, chilli and turmeric and the contrasting crunch of spring onions. Ideal with *parathe* or on toast.

Sabji refers to any vegetarian dish (mostly those cooked with *tarka*) and also means vegetables (*sabjia* = plural). Beans are vegetarian and are here cooked like vegetables, not like dhal, as they are cooked with a *tarka*, hence the name *sabji*.

SERVES 2 – 4

1 teaspoon oil	**a handful of chopped fresh coriander**
½ onion, chopped finely	**1 teaspoon garam masala**
1 garlic clove, chopped finely	**1 teaspoon salt**
1 teaspoon ground turmeric	**4 spring onions, sliced diagonally**
2 green chillies, chopped finely	**2 cans of baked beans**

1 Heat the oil and add the onion and garlic. Fry until lightly golden.

2 Add all the remaining ingredients except the baked beans and stir-fry for 3 minutes.

3 Add the baked beans, stir well and fry until heated through.

My cousin's little sons, Inderveer and Jasneal

DADDY'S EGG WRAP WITH HP SAUCE

My Dad invented this quite recently as a quick and portable meal. HP Sauce contains tamarind and is perfect to add a little zest to an omelette. Add a little garam masala and chopped fresh coriander and you have a tasty filling for a hot, delicious and healthy *roti* wrap. Add some salad and a dash of mango chutney and you're away.

SERVES 1

1 egg

a pinch of salt

a pinch of garam masala

a handful of frozen chopped fresh coriander

dollop of HP brown sauce

1 roti (page 158)

chopped salad, to serve

1 Beat the egg with the salt, garam masala, coriander and HP sauce.
2 Fry like an omelette in a pan.
3 Place on top of a *roti* and place some chopped salad in the middle.
4 Fold the wrap upwards from the bottom and inwards from the sides.

Sikh gentleman eating *Langar*

CHACHIJI'S NOODLES WITH KETCHUP

I distinctly remember eating this at my Chachiji's house when I was about 15. My cousins Amit, Anoop and I didn't feel like eating roti as we had eaten it all week, we wanted something different. Chachiji rustled up some outstanding noodles very similar to these. They were slightly sweet and sour, with mixed vegetables and flavoured with sugar, chilli and garlic. We ate steaming bowlfuls with lashings of tomato ketchup. Delicious. Chachiji also pointed out that I had always loved my food and that, when I was about four years old, I used to go to everyone's bowl in the room and pick out the cherries and grapes from their fruit cocktail for myself. I promise I don't do that anymore.

SERVES 4 – 6

2 tablespoons oil

1 teaspoon cumin seeds

½ onion, sliced thinly

2 garlic cloves, chopped finely

1 cup canned chopped tomatoes

1½ teaspoons salt

2 teaspoons light malt vinegar

½ teaspoon sugar

2 teaspoons dried red chilli flakes

3 cups of frozen diced mixed vegetables

250 g packet of egg noodles, cooked

garam masala, to serve

1 Heat the oil with the cumin seeds in a wok. When sizzling, add the onion and garlic. Fry until lightly golden.

2 Add the tomatoes, salt, vinegar, sugar and chilli and stir well for a couple of minutes.

3 Add the vegetables and stir-fry for 5 minutes.

4 Add the noodles and stir-fry for a further 5 minutes.

5 Sprinkle with garam masala to serve.

dhala *(dhaa-laa)*

LENTILS AND PULSES

Thomi mahaar dhal

(thoh·mee·ma·haar)

WASHED SPLIT URID LENTILS COOKED IN A PAN

I stayed with my grandparents for a few days when I was in my early teens and they asked me to make some dhal. I had never made dhal before and really didn't have a clue as to what I was doing so my Papiji gave me a helping hand to make this dhal (which is just as well, otherwise it would have been a real mush fest). I remember accidentally putting in a little too much turmeric, which made it neon yellow, but everyone was very kind and polite and ate it. Nowadays, my dhal tastes how it is supposed to taste and this recipe is for a dry version. It has a delicious hot oil, seasoned with asafoetida, ginger, garlic and ginger, poured over the top just before adding the onion slices to serve. It is wonderful and creamy and is best eaten with roti and a vegetable dish.

SERVES 4 – 6

1 cup thomi mahaar dhal (washed, split urid lentils), checked for stones and rinsed

2 teaspoons salt

½ teaspoon ground turmeric

½ cup oil + a little extra

1 large onion, chopped finely

4 garlic cloves, chopped finely

3 whole canned tomatoes, whizzed in a blender

1 tablespoon grated fresh root ginger

2 green chillies, chopped very finely

1 teaspoon garam masala

1 teaspoon asafoetida

2 handfuls of chopped fresh coriander

½ teaspoon sugar

a few very thin slices of onion, to garnish

1 Add 2 cups of cold water to the dhal and put on a medium heat. Add the salt and the turmeric and gently stir. Bring to the boil and then simmer for 30 minutes, adding more boiling water if necessary. The pan must not become dry.

2 Partly cover and simmer for a further 15 minutes.

3 Check the consistency, the dhal should be thick and even. Add more water if necessary and then fully cover and simmer for a further 15 minutes until dry and even textured.

4 Transfer the dhal to a pan in which a little oil has been heated. Stir-fry the dhal for a few minutes.

5 In a frying pan, heat the ½ cup of oil and add the onion and garlic. Fry until golden brown and then reduce the heat. Add the tomatoes, ginger, chillies, garam masala, asafoetida and a handful of coriander. Fry until nice and shiny. Add the sugar.

6 Pour the dry dhal into a serving dish. Pour the contents of the frying pan over the dhal.

7 Sprinkle with another handful of coriander and garnish with the onion slices.

Cooking with *Bhabiji* (my cousin's wife) and *Pooiji* (aunt)

Mahaar chole dhal

(ma-haar-sho-le)

URID BEANS AND SPLIT CHICK-PEAS COOKED IN A PRESSURE COOKER

Most British Asian households use a pressure-cooker to cook whole dhal as this really does speed up the entire process and allows you to get on with making other dishes at the same time. Therefore, when guests turn up, you can rustle up a dhal in 30 minutes instead of the usual hour and a half, making it a truly indispensable item. Take great care though. Back in the eighties my Mum's friend Davinder was rushing to try and get all the food ready for her impending guests and, without thinking, opened the lid of the pressure-cooker. Luckily, she wasn't injured but there was a huge dhal explosion and her guests arrived to see dhal on the walls, dhal on the floor, dhal on the ceiling and dhal all over poor old Davinder.

Superstition has it that you should not stir whole dhals upon placing them in the pan and adding water. It is thought to be bad luck, for the dhal probably, but I think this may be to do with not disturbing unsplit dhals until they have broken themselves during the cooking process. This runny dhal is a delicious combination of urid beans and split chick-peas and is finished with a *tarka* without tomato, giving it quite an earthy taste.

SERVES 4 – 6

½ cup saaf di mahaar dhal (whole urid beans), checked for stones and rinsed in warm water

½ cup chana dhal (split chick-peas), checked for stones and rinsed in warm water

2½ teaspoons salt

2 teaspoons ground turmeric

2 teaspoons oil

½ onion, chopped very finely

2 garlic cloves, chopped very finely

1 tablespoon grated fresh root ginger

2 green chillies, chopped finely

1 teaspoon garam masala

a handful of chopped fresh coriander

1 Fill the pressure-cooker pan with the drained dhal to the halfway mark with cold water.

2 Put the pan on a high heat. Add the salt and the turmeric. Stir the top of the water but not the dhal.

3 Put the lid on and wait until it has been brought to the boil (it should start to make a whistling noise and the little metal thing pops out).

4 Reduce the heat by half (often by putting the pan onto a smaller ring) and simmer for 30 minutes.

5 Turn off the heat and (very carefully – I use the handle of a wooden spoon) release the steam). Do not remove the lid!

6 Heat the oil in a frying pan and add the onion. A minute or so afterwards, add the garlic and fry until very lightly golden. Add the ginger and chillies and fry until golden brown, stirring all the while (most people do this part during the last 10 minutes of the dhal cooking).

7 Open the lid of the pressure-cooker and stir the dhal. Using a ladle, place a few ladlefuls of the dhal in the frying pan with the mixture (be careful, it will sizzle) and stir well. Pour the whole contents of the frying pan into the pan with the dhal. Stir well. Add the garam masala and stir well again. Sprinkle with coriander before serving.

Masoora di dhal

(ma-surra-dee)

RED SPLIT LENTILS COOKED IN A PAN

This lovely yellow dhal is most people's favourite, with its slightly nutty texture and tomato *tarka* and is quite a comfort food on cold days. This version has a thick, but still liquid, consistency and is topped with bright red chillies as a garnish. It is cooked a lot by Punjabis and is a real full-bodied no-nonsense dhal, just like the people. In fact, someone recently mentioned to me that they thought Punjabi mothers do not beat around the bush. My reply to that was 'Why should my mother beat around a bush when she has me to beat with her *chappal,* or quite often a rolling pin?'. Punjabi mothers, wouldn't change them for the world!

SERVES 4 — 6

½ cup moong dhal (whole mung beans), checked for stones and washed

½ cup masoor dhal (red split lentils), checked for stones and washed

1 teaspoon salt

1 teaspoon ground turmeric

2 teaspoons oil

½ onion, chopped very finely

1 garlic clove, chopped very finely

1 whole canned plum tomato and 1 tablespoon of juice, whizzed in a blender

1 teaspoon grated fresh root ginger

1 green chilli, finely chopped

½ teaspoon garam masala

To garnish:

a handful of chopped fresh coriander

2 red chillies, de-seeded and halved lengthways

1 Place the dhal in a large saucepan and fill to three-quarters full with boiling water.

2 Add the salt and place on a high heat.

3 Bring to the boil and reduce heat to a simmer. Using a large spoon, skim off all the scum on the surface.

4 Add the ground turmeric and stir well.

5 Partly cover and simmer for 30 minutes. Keep adding a little more boiling water if it starts to become too dry. It should be quite runny and even, not lentils floating in water.

6 Add 1 cup of boiling water and stir well.

7 After about 7 more minutes, switch off the heat.

8 Heat the oil in a frying pan and add the onion. After about 1 minute, add the garlic. When lightly golden add the tomato, ginger and chilli. Fry until it is a shiny, dry paste.

9 Pour into the pan with the dhal and mix well. Add the garam masala and stir well again. Garnish with coriander and the red chillies.

Saaf di masoor dhal

(saahf-dee-ma-surr)

WHOLE LENTILS COOKED IN A PRESSURE COOKER

This is my favourite dhal of all. Deep brown in colour with silky whole flat lentils, it is punctuated by bright green chilli and coriander. I often eat it with a large dollop of butter dropped into the centre of the bowl. It goes well with meat dishes as part of a full dinner and is also great with any rice and yoghurt. I prefer to eat it very simply though.

There is a scene in Shauna Singh Baldwin's moving novel set in the Punjab *What The Body Remembers* where they sit down to eat dhal and roti in the village. I was in London when I was reading it and my mouth was watering to eat this dhal just with plain roti and a little achaar. I continued to crave it until I was able to return home and eat this dhal cooked by my Mum. One of the simplest pleasures in life and yet one of the greatest.

SERVES 4 — 6

1 cup masoor dhal (whole brown/green lentils), checked for stones and washed

1½ teaspoons salt

1 teaspoon ground turmeric

2 tablespoons butter

½ onion, chopped very finely

1 garlic clove, chopped very finely

1 teaspoon grated fresh root ginger

1 green chilli, chopped finely

½ teaspoon garam masala

chopped fresh coriander

1 Fill the pressure-cooker pan, with the drained dhal, with boiling water to the halfway point. Add the salt and turmeric. Stir the water but not the lentils.

2 Replace the lid and bring to the boil. Simmer for 30 minutes.

3 Melt the butter in a frying pan and add the onion and garlic. Add the ginger and chilli and fry until golden brown.

4 Pour into the cooked dhal and gently mix in, leaving most of the *tarka* on the top. Sprinkle with the garam masala and with a handful of coriander before serving.

Mahaar mota di dhal

(ma-haar-mort-ha)
WHOLE URID AND MOTH BEANS COOKED IN A PAN

I have very strong attachments to this dhal. My parents told me when I was young the story of how they struggled when I was born, that they lived in a house with no other furniture than a small table and a rickety white chair and had no help or way to turn. They existed for a while on this dhal and white bread whilst striving to achieve and when I was tiny, it was what I was brought up on. Now, after working so hard their whole lives, keeping faith and remaining strong, my parents live comfortably but always say that during those hard times, no matter how little they had, they were happy and appreciated everything. That is what makes me appreciate this dhal.

SERVES 4 — 6

½ cup mahaar dhal (whole urid beans), checked for stones and washed

½ cup moth dhal (whole moth beans), checked for stones and washed

2 teaspoons salt

½ teaspoon ground turmeric

2 green chillies, chopped finely

3 whole canned plum tomatoes, whizzed in a blender

1 tablespoon grated fresh root ginger

½ cup oil

1 onion, chopped finely

4 garlic cloves, chopped very finely

1 teaspoon garam masala

chopped fresh coriander

1 Place the dhal in a large saucepan and add 7 cups of boiling water. Add the salt and turmeric, stir the water, though not the beans, and bring to the boil. Reduce the heat and simmer for 30 minutes.

2 Add the chillies, tomato and ginger to the pan. Stir gently and simmer for a further 30 minutes. Switch off the heat. The dhal should be runny like a soup but of an even consistency, with the dhal well blended with the water.

3 Heat the oil in a frying pan and fry the onion and garlic until lightly golden. Pour this *tarka* over the dhal and sprinkle with the garam masala and a handful of coriander.

Mahaar rongi di dhal

(ma-haar-ron-gee)

URID AND KIDNEY BEAN DHAL COOKED IN A PRESSURE-COOKER

This is a colourful and substantial dhal, the shiny maroon skins of the large kidney beans poking out from the smooth, chocolate-coloured dhal. Mahaar dhal, cooked on its own, is always the first item to be served at occasions such as weddings for good luck and is therefore highly revered. Superstition plays a large part in our lives and, boy, do we have some strange ones. I grew up getting a good slap round the back of my head if I sneezed before leaving the house as this meant something terrible was going to happen to us. We would all have to take our coats and shoes off and sit down for 10 minutes, pretending that we were not going out, to outwit the bad luck spirits, before quickly putting our coats and shoes back on again and hurrying out the door before getting caught out. I would also get told off for stepping over someone's feet if they were sitting down on the floor, as this is believed to stunt the person's growth. I would have to step back over the feet the other way to undo this bad luck. And throwing away any left over roti is bad luck for your mother, best feed it to the birds instead.

SERVES 4 — 6

½ cup mahaar dhal (whole urid beans), checked for stones and washed

½ cup rongi dhal (dried kidney beans), checked for stones and washed

1½ teaspoons salt

1 teaspoon ground turmeric

2 teaspoons oil

½ onion, chopped very finely

1 garlic clove, chopped very finely

1 teaspoon grated fresh root ginger

1 green chilli, chopped finely

1 teaspoon garam masala

chopped fresh coriander

1 Take the pressure-cooker pan with the dhal in and fill to the halfway mark with cold water. Add the salt and ground turmeric and stir the water, not the dhal.

2 When boiling, simmer for 30 minutes.

3 Heat the oil in a frying pan and add the onion. Fry gently for 1 minute and add the garlic. Add the ginger and chilli and fry until a golden, dry paste.

4 Add to the cooked dhal and stir well. Add the garam masala and stir well again. Sprinkle with a handful of coriander before serving.

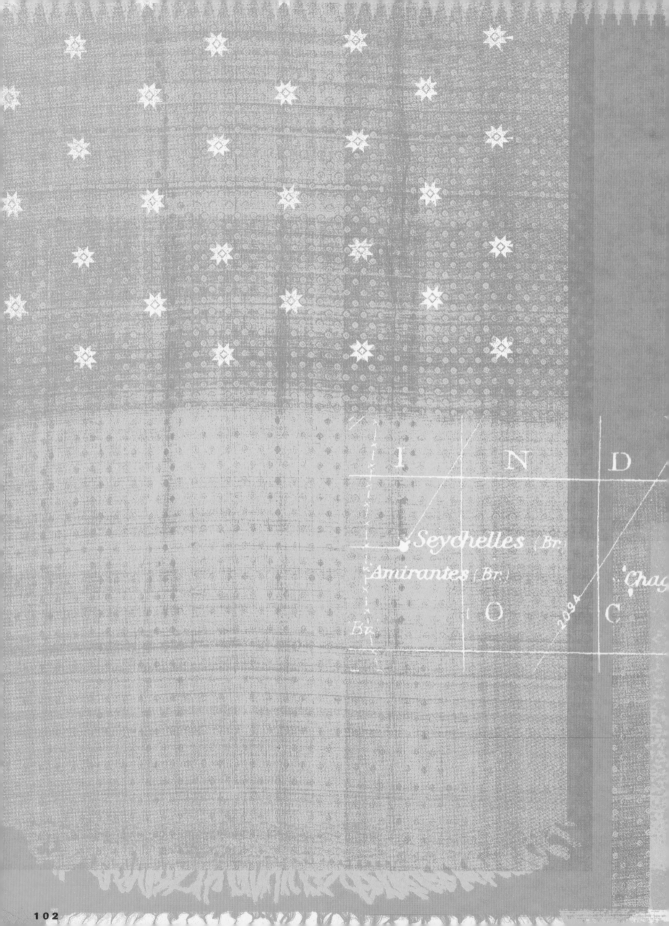

(kuhk-ree)

kukkri

CHICKEN DISHES

TANDOORI CHICKEN

This popular chicken is only really eaten at parties and weddings. I once had to make a huge vat full for my *Kash Mammaji's* (uncle's) wedding. My cousin, Nicky, and I had to skin about 100 chicken legs and I was plunged up to my elbows in a big yellow bucket with raw chicken flesh, which was so traumatising an experience that I swore off meat there and then. It didn't last long, though, as, when the chicken was cooked, it was simply too good to resist. This is actually very simple to make but always looks impressive at a dinner party or at a summer picnic. It looks as though you have slaved over it in the kitchen but really all you've done is put your feet up while it sits in the marinade.

MAKES 10 DRUMSTICKS

10 chicken drumsticks, skinned

1 tablespoon salt, plus a little to sprinkle

2 large cartons (500 g each) of set natural
   low-fat yogurt

3 tablespoons bottled lemon juice

4 garlic cloves, chopped finely

1 tablespoon grated fresh root ginger

4 tablespoons tandoori masala powder

3 green chillies, chopped finely

1 teaspoon + 4 tablespoons oil

2 teaspoons garam masala

2 teaspoons cumin seeds

1 whole lemon, cut into thin half-slices

5 red chillies, de-seeded and cut in half
   lengthways

½ small onion, sliced very thinly

fresh coriander sprigs, to garnish

1 Sprinkle the drumsticks with a little salt.

2 Pour the yogurt into a large mixing bowl and beat for a few minutes with a fork until it is of an even and creamy texture.

3 Add the tablespoon of salt, the lemon juice, garlic, ginger, tandoori masala powder, chillies, 1 teaspoon of oil and garam masala. Beat the mixture well with a fork.

4 Cut deep slits diagonally across the drumstick meat and place the chicken in the mixing bowl. Use your hands to rub the marinade well into the cuts in the chicken and make sure all the chicken is well coated.

5 Cover the bowl with clingfilm and refrigerate for at least 2 hours. Overnight is perfect.

6 Preheat the oven to 190°C/fan oven 170°C/Gas Mark 5. Remove the chicken legs and shake off any excess marinade. Place the drumsticks on a baking tray and cover tightly with foil.

7 Bake for about 1 hour until the chicken is cooked. Check by prodding the flesh with a knife, if the juice runs clear and the flesh is white not pink, it is done.

8 Remove the foil and brown the chicken under the grill or keep in the hottest part of the oven.

9 Just before serving, heat the 4 tablespoons of oil in a frying pan and add the cumin seeds. After 30 seconds, add the lemon slices, red chillies and onion. Fry on a high heat for a few minutes and then pour over the chicken. Garnish with coriander sprigs.

My Mum's thariwala chicken

(thurh-i-vaala)

CHICKEN WITH SAUCE

This is the classic chicken we eat at home. Delicious tender meat on the bone with soft potatoes soaked deeply in the rich onion and tomato sauce, shimmering with chicken juices. We often eat this dish on a Saturday evening with vegetable rice, *tharwala dahi* (page 175), *roti*, freshly cut salad and a good dose of *achaar*. My Dad always makes sure that, with the hustle and bustle of today's lifestyle, we sit down and have a proper meal on a Saturday night, which is often coupled with watching Blind Date. We simply call this chicken with rice 'meat and *chaul*' and it is often served to us when we visit relatives too. We would always have it when we visited *Bindi Massi* (my aunt), followed by a delicious Sarah Lee cheesecake.

In days gone by, meat was often not eaten during the rest of the week so this weekend meal was always a bit special and to cook meat for guests, even if it is with dhal and vegetable *sabji* too, is the done thing.

SERVES 4

2 tablespoons oil

1 large onion, chopped finely

1 garlic clove, chopped finely

1 cup canned chopped tomatoes, whizzed in
  a blender

2 teaspoons grated fresh root ginger

2 green chillies, chopped finely

1½ teaspoons salt

1 teaspoon ground turmeric

2 teaspoons garam masala

2 handfuls of chopped fresh coriander

2 chicken legs

2 potatoes, peeled and quartered

1 Cut the chicken legs into two drumsticks and two thighs. Cut the thighs in half. Wash, skin and trim of excess fat.

2 Heat the oil in a large saucepan and add the onions and garlic. Fry until a rich golden brown (onions should be a darker brown than they are in vegetable dishes).

3 Turn the heat down and add the tomatoes and ½ cup of cold water. Stir well.

4 Add the ginger, chillies, salt, ground turmeric, garam masala and a good handful of coriander.

5 Stir well to keep crushing the onions into the tomatoes. When the mixture has become shiny and the oil separates, add the chicken. Coat well with mixture.

6 Turn the heat up high and stir-fry for 5 minutes.

7 Add enough boiling water to fill the pan to three-quarters full and totally cover the chicken.

8 Bring to the boil, turn the heat down, partly cover and simmer for 10 minutes.

9 Add the potatoes, stir gently, bring to the boil again and simmer for a further 25 minutes with the pan covered. Sprinkle with another handful of coriander before serving.

DEVILISH BUTTER CHICKEN

This is a very simple version of the widely loved butter chicken. It is probably the first chicken dish you should try if you are not very confident with cooking meat, as it is very easy and the results will win you applause. You'll have people eating out of your hands in no time! It is very rich, though, so make sure you serve it with something simple like a salad and some chutney to add a little zest. And remember, you can always start your diet tomorrow!

SERVES 2 — 4

125 g (4½ oz) salted butter

4 drops of red food colouring

450 g (1 lb) skinless, boneless chicken breasts,
    cut into bite-size pieces

a pinch of garam masala

fresh coriander sprigs, to garnish

1 Melt the butter very gently on a low heat in a saucepan.

2 Add the food colouring and stir into the butter.

3 Add the chicken and the garam masala.

4 Cover and cook gently, stirring occasionally until the chicken is cooked (about 15 minutes) and has absorbed all the liquid and only butter solids remain in the pan.

5 Remove the chicken with a slotted spoon to a dish. Garnish with coriander sprigs.

Arranged Marriages

The image of arranged marriages is long out of date. Non-Asians imagine a scenario where the parents choose a boy for their daughter without her consent. Seeing him for the first time on her wedding day, she is packed off to a life of servitude with a person she doesn't know. That may have been the case twenty years ago. I recently explained the modern process to a friend of mine. Basically, parents nowadays discuss requirements with the girl and, only with her consent, begin looking for someone who is the appropriate religion, caste, from a good family and everything the girl wants in term s of height, looks, career and location. They will do this through asking family members and word circulates on the Indian network, which operates like a very slick recruitment agency.

The girl will receive photographs and if she approves of any of them, she will meet the person and his family at her parents' home. They will then get the opportunity to speak alone and if all goes well there will be a series of meetings until they decide they do or do not want to marry each other. The girl can reject as many times as she likes and there is little pressure. It may sound clinical but with non-Asian divorce rates soaring and so many women unable to find Mr Right, it is actually very effective. By the end of the conversation, my sceptical friend was asking if my parents could look for her too!

GREEN MASALA ROAST CHICKEN

Everyone should try this version of whole roast chicken. With a warm aromatic fragrance and mild taste, this chicken is marinated and then roasted in a green crust of cracked coriander seed, saffron, ginger, garlic, lemon and fresh green chilli. This is very easy to make, looks outstanding and is perfect for guests who are not too sure about Indian food. Served with roast potatoes, Oven-baked Cherry Tomatoes with Saffron (page 82) and gravy, this is a roast dinner like you've never had before. The cold chicken leftovers are also lovely in thick granary bread with salad as a gourmet sandwich.

SERVES 4 – 6

1 whole chicken without giblets, skinned	**2 tablespoons whole coriander seeds**
2 teaspoons salt	**2 teaspoons garam masala**
2 tablespoons lemon juice	**6 garlic cloves, chopped roughly**
4 tablespoons oil	**1 small onion, chopped roughly**
½ teaspoon saffron strands	**1 tablespoon grated fresh root ginger**
4 green chillies	**1 teaspoon natural low-fat set yogurt**
1½ teaspoons ground turmeric	**1 lemon, cut in thick wedges, to garnish**

1 Put the chicken in a steamer or a colander over a saucepan of simmering water, cover and steam for 10 minutes.

2 Meanwhile, place all the remaining ingredients in a blender and whizz until you have a nice smooth paste.

3 Drain the water from the chicken, stab all over with a knife and place in a baking tray.

4 Rub the paste all over the chicken, into the cuts and inside the chicken.

5 Cover the tray with cling film and refrigerate for 30 minutes. Preheat the oven to 220°C/fan oven 200°C/Gas Mark 7

6 Remove the cling film, cover with foil and cook in the oven for 1 hour.

7 Remove the foil and continue to cook until the chicken is browned.

8 Garnish with the lemon wedges.

POOIJI'S SUBLIME CHICKEN

This is a sizzling sweet-and-sour-flavoured chicken dish with just a little sauce. This is best served with a dhal (*masoora di dhal*, page 98 goes well) and *roti* although this is also great in pitta pockets with salad.

SERVES 4 – 6

¾ cup oil

1 teaspoon cumin seeds

2 cloves

2 onions, chopped roughly

4 garlic cloves, chopped roughly

4 canned plum tomatoes, whizzed in a blender

3 green chillies, chopped finely

1½ teaspoons salt

2 teaspoons grated fresh root ginger

1 teaspoon garam masala

2 teaspoons ground turmeric

½ teaspoon tandoori masala powder

450 g (1 lb) skinless, boneless chicken thighs, chopped and fat removed.

1 red pepper, de-seeded and sliced thinly lengthways

8 mushrooms, sliced

1 small onion, cut into eighths

1 teaspoon vinegar

1 teaspoon tomato ketchup

1 teaspoon sugar

a handful of chopped fresh coriander

1 Heat the oil in a large saucepan and add the cumin seeds and cloves. When the cumin seeds are sizzling, add the onion and garlic. Turn the heat down very low, cover and cook for 10 minutes.

2 Turn the heat off. Remove the onions with a slotted spoon, leaving the oil in the pan, and place in a blender. Whizz until smooth. Place the pan with the oil back on a medium heat. When the oil is heated, return the onions to the pan. Stir well and fry until deep golden brown – but not burnt!

3 Turn the heat down and add the tomatoes, salt, ginger, garam masala, turmeric and tandoori masala. Stir well and add a splash of water. Cook until shiny and the oil separates.

4 Add the chicken and stir well to coat. Cover and cook on a low heat for 30 minutes, stirring occasionally. Add the pepper, mushrooms and onion and ¾ cup of boiling water. Stir-fry for 10 minutes.

5 Combine the vinegar, tomato ketchup and sugar in a bowl. Add to the chicken and stir thoroughly. Fry for 30 seconds. Sprinkle with a handful of coriander before serving.

A delicious dish being cooked at an authentic restaurant

BINDI MASSI'S BAKED MILLENNIUM CHICKEN

My **Bindi Massi** (aunt) made this for us on New Year's Eve 1999. The occasion prompted a special chicken dish and so we were treated to chicken, potatoes and onion in a thick tomato-based sauce baked in the oven and then browned on top and garnished with coriander. This method gave the meat and vegetables a wonderful roasted taste and a darkened visual effect and went down a treat with lightly fried rice. As the clock struck and, glued to the BBC countdown, we suddenly all realised we should have planned to be in Trafalgar Square for the millennium celebrations, my cousins Sapphire and Areese ran outdoors to see the fireworks and I went back into the kitchen for seconds.

SERVES 6 – 8

2 tablespoons oil

1 large onion, chopped finely

2 garlic cloves, chopped finely

2 cups chopped canned tomatoes, whizzed in a
　blender

2 teaspoons grated fresh root ginger

4 green chillies, chopped finely

2 teaspoons salt

2 teaspoons ground turmeric

2 teaspoons garam masala

a handful of chopped fresh coriander

4 drumsticks and 4 chicken thighs, skinned and
　trimmed of excess fat

1 small onion, cut into rings

1　Preheat the oven to 200°C/fan oven 180°C/Gas Mark 6. Heat the oil in a large saucepan and add the onion and garlic.

2　When deep golden brown, turn down the heat and add the tomatoes and stir well.

3　Add the ginger, chillies, salt, turmeric, garam masala, coriander and a splash of water. Cook until shiny and the oil separates.

4　Turn up the heat and add the chicken. Stir-fry for 5 minutes. Add the onion rings and stir well.

5　Transfer the contents of the pan to a large baking dish. Sprinkle with more coriander and cover tightly with foil.

6　Cook on a medium heat about for one hour until the chicken is cooked and tender.

7　Remove the foil and brown the chicken.

CHICKEN WITH WILTED BABY SPINACH

Baby spinach leaves are so mild and easy to cook, adding colour and texture to dishes immediately. This simple dish has a thick sauce of saffron, garlic, ginger and tomato; the wilted whole spinach leaves snaking their way around the tender, boneless, bite-size pieces of chicken. It is fantastic with *parathe* or *pooria* (page 160 or 168) and *bhoondiwala dahi* (page 180).

SERVES 4 – 6

¾ cup oil

1 teaspoon cumin seeds

2 onions, grated

4 garlic cloves, crushed

4 whole canned plum tomatoes, whizzed in
   a blender

3 green chillies, chopped finely

1½ teaspoons salt

2 teaspoons grated fresh root ginger

1 teaspoon garam masala

2 teaspoons ground turmeric

2 or 3 saffron strands

450 g (1 lb) skinless, boneless chicken,
   chopped and excess fat removed

¼ teaspoon white sugar

a packet of baby spinach leaves

a handful of chopped fresh coriander

1 Heat the oil in a large saucepan with the cumin seeds. When they are sizzling, add the onion and garlic. Stirring well, fry until a deep golden brown.

2 Turn the heat down and add the tomatoes, chillies, salt, ginger, garam masala, turmeric and saffron. Add a splash of water and cook well until the mixture is shiny and the oil separates.

3 Add the chicken and stir thoroughly to coat with the mixture.

4 Cover with a lid and simmer on a low heat for 10 minutes.

5 Add ½ cup of boiling water and simmer again, covered, on a low heat for 10 further minutes.

6 Stir well, add the sugar and whole spinach leaves and simmer covered for a further 10 minutes. Sprinkle with a handful of coriander before serving.

BAKED LEMON CHICKEN

I was making chicken fajitas one evening and accidentally dropped the wedge of lemon I was squeezing into the chicken and pepper mixture. I was distracted and forgot to take it out and so it sizzled away with the chicken, vegetables and spices. My Dad happened to get the piece of lemon in his fajita and commented that it had become soft, tasted like *achaar* and was surprisingly nice with the chicken. I therefore decided to make a dish in which we use the whole fruit of the lemon with the meat instead of just adding the juice. This dish combines chicken on the bone with thin slices of lemon that become meltingly soft with the meat juices when baked in the oven. It is quite a fiery and tangy dish and so is best served with plain rice or *bhature* (page 169) and plain *dahi*.

SERVES 4

1 onion, chopped finely

2 garlic cloves, chopped finely

4 tablespoons oil

1 cup canned chopped tomatoes

1 teaspoon ground turmeric

2 teaspoons garam masala

1½ teaspoons salt

3 green chillies, chopped finely

2 teaspoons grated fresh root ginger

a large handful of chopped fresh coriander

1 lemon, cut in thin slices and then halved
   again

4 chicken thighs, skinned, trimmed of excess
   fat and scored across the top

fresh coriander sprigs, to garnish

1   Preheat the oven to 200°C/fan oven 180°C/Gas Mark 6. Heat the oil in a pan and add the onions and garlic. Fry until a deep golden brown. Turn the heat down and add the tomatoes. Stir well.

2   Add the turmeric, garam masala, salt, chillies, ginger and a large handful of coriander.

3   Add ¼ cup of boiling water. When shiny and the oil has separated, turn off the heat. Add 1½ cups of boiling water. Stir well.

4   Cover the bottom of a large baking dish with the lemon slices. Place the chicken on top.

5   Pour the onion mixture over the chicken to coat the pieces fully.

6   Cover with foil and cook in the oven for 30 minutes.

7   Remove the foil and cook for a further 15 minutes.

8   Stir well and cook for a final 15 minutes.

9   Garnish with coriander sprigs.

BADA-SINGH CHICKEN MEATBALLS

We call meatballs *kofte* and usually have the lamb or vegetarian variants. These delicious balls of flavour demonstrate the versatility of chicken mince and are little bombs ready to explode with ginger, cumin and coriander flavours. Served in little bowls with *rotia*, they make a wondrous evening meal and are also great tossed with spaghetti.

SERVES 4 — 6

For the kofte:

450 g (1 lb) chicken mince

2 teaspoons grated fresh root ginger

1 teaspoon cumin seeds

1 small onion, grated

1 teaspoon salt

a small handful of chopped fresh coriander

For the masala:

¾ cup oil

1 teaspoon cumin seeds

2 cloves

1 bay leaf

2 onions, chopped roughly

4 garlic cloves, chopped roughly

4 canned plum tomatoes, whizzed in a blender

3 green chillies, chopped finely

1½ teaspoons salt

2 teaspoons grated fresh root ginger

1 teaspoon garam masala

2 teaspoons ground turmeric

½ teaspoon tandoori masala powder

¼ teaspoon sugar

a handful of chopped fresh coriander

1 Combine all the meatball ingredients together with a fork in a large mixing bowl. Divide the mixture into small equally sized balls.

2 Heat the oil in a large saucepan, with the cumin seeds, cloves and bay leaf. When sizzling, add the onions and garlic. Cover and cook on a very low heat for 10 minutes.

3 Turn off the heat. Using a slotted spoon, transfer the onion mixture to a blender, leaving the oil in the pan. Whizz till smooth.

4 Return the pan to the heat and, when the oil is hot again, return the onion mixture to the pan. Stir well. Fry until a deep golden brown.

5 Turn the heat down and add the tomatoes, chillies, salt, ginger, garam masala and turmeric. When shiny and the oil separates, add 3 cups of boiling water and stir well.

6 Gently lower the meatballs into the pan, cover and simmer on a low heat for 30 minutes. Gently shake the pan occasionally to make sure neither the sauce nor the meatballs are sticking to the bottom, but do not stir!

7 Very gently turn the meatballs over, sprinkle in the tandoori masala and the sugar, shake the pan gently and continue to cook with the lid off for 5 minutes until the sauce has thickened a little.

8 Sprinkle with a handful of coriander before serving.

DADDY'S CREAMY CHICKEN

My Dad is a great experimenter in the kitchen and has a boundless enthusiasm for food. He is always looking for new combinations to try and my Mum, brother, sister and I are the lucky tasters of any new creations. This is one of the dishes that went down particularly well. It is fascinating how a couple of simple additions can transform a dish completely. The additions of cream, lime juice and mango chutney form a succulent melody of a dish with a zesty top note, creamy middle note and a fruity base note. It is a delicious treat and goes well with any rice and *dahi* with lots of freshly chopped salad.

SERVES 4

2 teaspoons oil

1 onion, chopped finely

1 garlic clove, chopped finely

1 cup canned chopped tomatoes, whizzed in
   a blender

2 green chillies, chopped finely

3 teaspoons grated fresh root ginger

½ teaspoons ground turmeric

4 teaspoons garam masala

2 teaspoons salt

2 handfuls of chopped fresh coriander

450 g (1 lb) boneless, skinless chicken, diced

½ x 142 ml carton of single cream

1 tablespoon mango chutney

juice of 1 lime

1 Heat the oil in a saucepan and add the onion and garlic. Fry until a deep golden brown.

2 Turn the heat down and add the tomatoes, chilli, ginger, turmeric, garam masala, salt and a handful of coriander. Add a splash of water and cook until all the ingredients are well blended.

3 When the mixture is shiny and the oil separates, add the chicken pieces.

4 Stir-fry for 10 minutes.

5 Add 4 cups of boiling water and bring to the boil.

6 Reduce to a simmer and stir in the cream, mango chutney and lime juice.

7 Leave to simmer on a low heat, covered, for 30 minutes. Add splashes of extra boiling water if it becomes a little too dry. Sprinkle with more coriander before serving.

laal gosht

(laal-gorsht)

RED MEATS

Keema

(kee-mah)

MINCED LAMB

Minced lamb is inexpensive and this dish shows off all its most desirable qualities. The mince should be moist and juicy; it is brought to life by the simple *tarka* and then given a good sprinkling of peas. Fresh, hot and quick, it is just what you need for supper when you have come in from the cold. This is one of my sister, Karen's, favourites but, instead of eating it with buttery *rotia* and *achaar* as I do, she uses it as a rich topping for jacket potatoes, accompanied with crunchy salad.

SERVES 4 — 6

2 tablespoons oil	1½ teaspoons salt
1 onion, chopped finely	1 teaspoon garam masala
1 garlic clove, chopped finely	2 handfuls of chopped fresh coriander
½ cup canned chopped tomatoes	450 g (1 lb) lean minced lamb
1 teaspoon grated fresh root ginger	2 cups of frozen peas
2 green chillies, chopped finely	

1 Heat the oil in a large saucepan and add the onion and garlic. Fry until a deep golden brown.

2 Turn the heat down and add the tomatoes, ginger, chillies, salt, garam masala and a handful of coriander.

3 When the mixture has become shiny and the oil separates, add the mince.

4 Stir thoroughly to coat. Add the peas and stir thoroughly again. Stir-fry for a few minutes.

5 Add 1 cup of boiling water and bring to the boil. Reduce to a low heat, cover and cook for 20 minutes.

6 Take the lid off, turn the heat up and stir-fry for a few minutes. The lamb should be moist but there should be no water left. Serve scattered with more chopped coriander.

Daddy's thariwala lamb

(thuh-ri-vaala)

LAMB WITH SAUCE

We don't eat lamb very often, most Sikh families tend to eat more chicken than any other meat, but Muslim families eat lamb much more frequently. When we do eat lamb at home it feels like an expensive treat and I simply adore it. My Dad makes the best lamb in the world and this recipe is for a version with small, silky boneless morsels of tender lamb in a sea of aromatic sauce tinged with lime. It goes outstandingly well with Wild Rice with Cashews and plenty of *tharwala dahi* (pages 147 and 175). My Dad explained to me that he finds some restaurant lamb dishes have an unpleasant smell, which is caused by the excess fat. Therefore, my Dad's version includes browning the lamb first and discarding this fat to create a healthier, fresher and much more pleasantly smelling dish.

SERVES 4 — 6

800 g (1¾ lb) boneless leg of lamb, skinned, cut into small cubes, fat trimmed off

2½ tablespoons oil

1 large onion, chopped finely

1 garlic clove, chopped finely

1 cup canned chopped tomatoes, whizzed in a blender

½ teaspoon ground turmeric

1 tablespoon grated fresh root ginger

2 green chillies, chopped finely

1½ teaspoons salt

4 teaspoons garam masala

2 handfuls of chopped fresh coriander

juice of ½ lime

1 Gently heat a large frying pan. Place the cubes of lamb in the pan and cook on a low to medium heat, until there is no pink flesh to be seen. When the lamb is pale brown all over, turn off the heat. Discard the fat by draining the meat in a colander.

2 Heat the oil in a large saucepan and add the onion and garlic. Fry until a deep golden brown.

3 Turn the heat down and add the tomatoes, turmeric, ginger, chillies, salt, garam masala, a handful of coriander and a good splash of water.

4 When the mixture has become shiny and the oil separates, add the lamb.

5 Stir thoroughly to coat with the mixture. Stir-fry for 5 minutes.

6 Add the lime juice and 3 cups of boiling water. Bring to the boil.

7 Reduce the heat and simmer, covered, on a low heat for 35 minutes. Sprinkle with more coriander before serving.

LAMB CHOP MASALA

The trick with this is to make sure the lamb is tender; you don't want it chewy and rubbery like an old *chappal*! This is a very impressive dinner-party dish, as not only does it look magnificent, it tastes divine. It has its roots in Mughal culture; such dishes, mostly cooked by Pakistanis and Arabs today, often require puréed garlic and ginger, as this one does. Do not rush the cooking, take your time. Do not rush the eating of it either; this deserves to be savoured slowly.

These chops are cooked gently in a smooth sauce to which grated ginger and butter is added in the final stages to impart extra heat and opulence. The topping of red onion, spring onion and coriander adds a wonderful dash of colour. Eat with thick soft *bhature* and *bhoondiwala dahi* (pages 169 and 180) for a luxurious meal.

SERVES 4

2 teaspoons grated fresh root ginger, defrosted if frozen	½ teaspoon red chilli powder
	½ teaspoon ground turmeric
2 teaspoons chopped garlic	2 tablespoons grated fresh root ginger
4 tablespoons oil	25 g (1 oz) butter
450 g (1 lb) fresh, not-too-ripe tomatoes, chopped finely	*To garnish:*
	¼ red onion, sliced very thinly
4 lamb chops	1 spring onion, chopped finely
1 teaspoon salt	a handful of chopped fresh coriander

1 Purée the ginger and garlic in a mini blender or by pounding them in a mortar with a pestle, until smooth. Heat the oil in a large saucepan and add the ginger and garlic. Fry until a deep golden brown.

2 Turn the heat down and add the tomatoes. Fry for 1 minute.

3 Add the lamb chops, salt, red chilli powder, turmeric and 600 ml (1 pint) of boiling water.

4 Stir well and cook on a low heat, covered, for 50 minutes. Add a little more boiling water if it begins to get dry.

5 Take off the lid and turn the heat up to evaporate any excess water.

6 Turn the heat down low and keep stirring until the oil separates from the sauce. You should be left with a thick sauce.

7 Add the ginger and butter. Stir and cook uncovered for about 4 minutes.

8 Garnish with the red onion, spring onion and coriander.

Dhaniya lamb

(dhun-ee-ya)

LAMB WITH CORIANDER

Coriander works very well here as its fresh and clean taste revives the deepness of the lamb and looks wonderful glistening away, emerald green, in the pan. Dense quantities of coriander leaf can be quite harsh on the stomach, though, so eat a reasonable, not huge, portion and always couple it with lashings of plain *dahi*.

SERVES 4

3 tablespoons oil

1 large onion, grated

2 garlic cloves, chopped finely

1 cup canned chopped tomatoes, whizzed in
   a blender

½ teaspoon ground turmeric

1 tablespoon finely chopped fresh root ginger

2 green chillies, finely chopped

1½ teaspoons salt

4 teaspoons garam masala

2 large bunches of fresh coriander, chopped
   finely

450 g (1 lb) lean boneless lamb, cubed

1 Heat the oil in a large saucepan and add the onion and garlic. Fry until deep golden brown.

2 Turn the heat down and add the tomatoes, turmeric, ginger, chillies, salt and garam masala. Stir well and add ½ cup of boiling water. Add the coriander. Cook until the mixture has become shiny and the oil separates.

3 Add the lamb and stir-fry for 5 minutes.

4 Add 1 cup of boiling water and stir well. Cover and simmer on a low heat for 30 minutes until the meat is tender and a thick sauce remains.

My Mum makes the best food in the world as far as I'm concerned and therefore she was the inspiration for the book. Watch those hands go!

Indian Restaurant Food

I grew up really confused about Indian restaurants in this country. When I was young I could not understand why the food served up in such establishments was labelled as Indian – it bore no resemblance to anything I ate at home. I have admiration for the Indians who came over to this country in the 50s and 60s and with an entrepreneurial spirit set up restaurants serving Indian food to the West. It was so loved that it is now Britain's most popular dish. There are some fantastic Indian restaurants now, it is just that no matter how nice the food, it is still worlds away from home cooking. The tastes, smells, textures are all so different.

I have spoken to many Indian restaurant chefs around the country about why the food is so different from the food we cook at home. They were completely honest and explained that, back when the first Indian restaurants in England appeared, there were no rules. There were no real Indian grocers and so they used little in the way of fresh ingredients. Powders were cheap and long lasting and chefs used powdered garlic, ginger, coriander, onion and chilli. A lot of Indian restaurants still do. They make a base of tomato and oil which forms the basic sauce for every dish and they add a little more chilli or maybe some cream depending on what the dish requires. After all, the more sauces you make, the more skilled manpower you require, all of whom need a wage. Due to its high oil content this base keeps well in the refrigerator and can be frozen in large batches. It makes frying spices less difficult; because there is more oil, the spices don't stick and so less stirring is needed freeing chefs up to get on with something else. New dishes were invented to add variety, such as Chicken Tikka Masala, which was invented for English restaurant-goers because Chicken Tikka was so popular. These early chefs were right to do whatever they could to maintain their business and so the dishes were adapted to make them more palatable to Western tastes. Most British people could not eat anything spicy and so dishes were created with lots of cream, making them mild and sweet, like the restaurant version of the Korma. But restaurants also catered for macho tastes at the other extreme and created very fiery dishes with red chilli powder and little else.

Often the names of the dishes would be real but the actual food was far from how it is made in India. The diversity of all the cuisines of India became condensed into one single sauce sitting frozen in restaurant freezers. Restaurant staff, as they explained to me, would never eat this food themselves. In fact, one Bengali chef said he invented so many dishes but ate broken rice and simple fish for his own lunchtime. Put simply by another restaurant owner, 'The English didn't know any different and they liked it. For us it was cheap and easy so it was good for everyone. But in areas where there are lots of Indians, such as Southall, you have to make food properly. You couldn't get away with it there. There would be uproar'.

ROAST LAMB DESI STYLE

There is something very rustic and pastoral about a whole joint of meat slowly cooked, the aroma filtering throughout the house, and then carved at the centre of the table. This recipe harks back to an older age when marinating and slow cooking were the best and cheapest methods available. The lamb is treated with red chilli, garam masala, ginger, garlic, tandoori masala powder and lime to give it a piquant crispiness on the outside, offering contrast to the pinky sweet lamb inside. This can be served as part of a roast dinner, with new potatoes tossed in mint leaves and cumin seeds, Maharajah's Mash (page 84) or simply with fresh crusty bread and Tomato and Onion Chutney (page 174).

SERVES 6

2.25 kg (5 lb) leg of lamb, washed and stabbed all over with a large knife

For the paste:

3 tablespoons grated fresh root ginger, defrosted if frozen

3 tablespoons chopped garlic

1 tablespoon dried red chilli flakes

2 tablespoons garam masala

2 tablespoons salt

1 teaspoon tandoori masala powder

lime juice

1 Blend the ginger and garlic in a mini blender or by pounding them in a mortar with a pestle until smooth. Mix the chilli, garam masala, ginger, garlic, salt, tandoori masala powder and a dash of lime juice in a bowl with a fork. Rub the mixture into the lamb, pressing into the cuts. Wrap with clingfilm and leave to marinate overnight.

2 Preheat the oven to 170°C/fan oven 150°C/Gas Mark 3.

3 Unwrap the lamb and place in a baking tray. Cover tightly with foil. Place in the oven and cook for about 2 hours.

4 Remove the foil and raise the oven temperature to around 200°C/fan oven 180°C/Gas Mark 6. Cook for another 30 minutes or long enough to brown the lamb all over.

GRILLED LAMB CHOPS

Whenever I do go out to eat at Indian restaurants, these are always what I have. It really is a sight to watch me eat lamb chops, I love them so much that I unintentionally go at them like an animal crazed with starvation and I always get a gentle nudge to remember my manners. I love the way they are soaked throughout with the yogurt, chilli, lemon and spices, the marinade tenderising the meat and mingling with the lamb juices, and are then grilled over open flames for a chargrilled effect. Of course you can use a regular grill but a barbecue will give the maximum impact. I have also added a ginger, tomato and onion dressing which is heated through and poured over at the last minute to make them sizzle.

SERVES 4

3 tablespoons natural set low-fat yogurt	3 tablespoons oil
1 teaspoon dried red chilli flakes	1 teaspoon grated fresh root ginger
1 tablespoon lemon juice	1 tomato, chopped finely
1 teaspoon salt	¼ onion, chopped finely
1 teaspoon tandoori masala powder	a handful of chopped fresh coriander
4 lamb chops	

1 Beat the yogurt, chilli, lemon juice, salt and the tandoori masala powder together in a bowl with a fork.

2 Rub into the lamb chops. Place the chops in a dish and cover with clingfilm. Marinate for 2 hours minimum.

3 Grill the lamb chops until brown and fully cooked, about 15 minutes, turning frequently. Place in a serving dish.

4 Heat the oil in a frying pan and add the ginger, tomato and onion. Stir-fry for 5 minutes and then pour over the lamb chops. Sprinkle with a handful of coriander before serving.

SIZZLING STEAK FILLETS

I once had a conversation with my lovely friend Louise that really left me thinking about steak. I had never eaten it before and absentmindedly pointed this out whilst our friend Bernie tucked into her steak baguette at lunch. Louise then brought this up at a later point when we were in a burger joint as she genuinely found it strange that, as I had been born in this country, I had never eaten steak before in my whole life. So I thought about why and asked around. Most of my British-Asian friends had never eaten steak either, mainly because our parents didn't eat beef (the cow is sacred to Hindus and is generally revered in India by Hindus and Sikhs alike) and so didn't cook it at home. Another reason was that it was thought to be too expensive. Some of my British-Asian friends who did eat beef said they'd never wanted to eat steak because it was regarded as a posh English dish, which involved eating meat with blood still in it, and claimed they'd rather stick to their Big Macs, thanks. I was intrigued and so decided to try it. So here is my version of steak fillets, in honour of my friend Louise. Marinated beef steaks which are then grilled or fried to your liking from rare to well done. I have to say, they went down a storm in my house and we also ate them sliced into thin strips, stir-fried with peppers, onions and lime and served in tortillas with Tomato and Onion Chutney (page 174) and crème fraîche. Superb.

SERVES 2

2 beef frying steaks, weighing about 125 g (4 oz) each

10 tablespoons natural set low-fat yogurt

1 teaspoon salt

2 teaspoons garam masala

1 tablespoon lemon juice

1 garlic clove, sliced very thinly

¼ onion, sliced very thinly

½ teaspoon red chilli powder

1 tablespoon grated fresh root ginger

a handful of chopped fresh coriander

2 tablespoons oil

1 Using a mallet, beat the steaks to thin them out.

2 Beat the remaining ingredients (except the oil) together with a fork in a mixing bowl. Add the steaks and massage the marinade into them. Cover the bowl with clingfilm and leave to marinate overnight.

3 Heat the oil in a large frying pan or heat a griddle pan. Shake off excess marinade. Fry or grill the steaks on a high heat for 5 minutes, turning over frequently.

4 Brown the steaks to your liking.

Me picking out vegetables

VERY HOT DOGS

Muslims do not eat pork and most Hindus are vegetarian but a lot of Sikhs are partial to a good sausage and bacon fry-up at the weekends. Hot dogs are fun and popular with children and adults alike so here is my version: hot-dog-style pork kebabs made with three types of chilli (fresh green, dried red and pickled) to give a little kick, served in hot dog buns and topped with fried onions and Ten-Second Yogurt and Mint Chutney (page 176). Delicious as picnic or barbecue food.

MAKES 10

450 g (1 lb) pork mince, not lean

2 green chillies, chopped finely

4 pickled green chillies, chopped finely

½ teaspoon dried red chilli flakes

1 garlic clove, chopped finely

2 teaspoons grated fresh root ginger

1 teaspoon garam masala

1 teaspoon salt

1 teaspoon tomato ketchup

a dash of lemon juice

1 Combine all the ingredients together in a large mixing bowl using a fork.

2 Divide the mixture into 10 equal portions and make into sausage shapes.

3 Grill or cook in an oven until brown.

MASALA BURGERS

My Dad used to make the most succulent, thick, fresh home-made burgers when I was younger, frying them on the *thawa*. These are ideal for burger-lovers who are looking for something a little different. Making the burgers is a pleasure in itself, shaping the mixture together with your hands and then slapping them onto a hot, sizzling griddle. I served these at a dinner party recently on their own without the bread and they were fully enjoyed with rice and chutney. Serve as you wish, in buns with relish and a little mozzarella, chopped up and stuffed in a pitta with onions or simply with salad.

MAKES 8

450 g (1 lb) lamb or beef mince, not lean

1 garlic clove, chopped finely

1 small onion, grated and squeezed

1 tablespoon grated fresh root ginger

3 green chillies, chopped finely

¼ teaspoon coriander seeds, crushed

a handful of chopped fresh coriander

1 teaspoon salt

1 teaspoon garam masala

1 Mix all the ingredients together with a fork in a large mixing bowl.

2 Divide the mixture into eight equal portions, shape into balls and then flatten into patties.

3 Grill or fry until cooked to your liking.

(ma-chi) *machchi*

FISH

DEEP-FRIED FISH NUGGETS

I first tried these when I was 16 and was overawed by the pungent flavours that are a real disco party for the taste buds. I watched as the taut cod flesh was marinated in carom, cumin and coriander seeds with chilli, lime, garlic and yogurt and then plunged into a sea of hot oil, to emerge as sparkling, sunset-orange chunks which you just had to put in your mouth. Punjabis don't eat much fish but, when they do, boy do they make it well. Eat with lots of skinny fries and a drizzle of Ten-Second Yogurt and Mint Chutney (page 176) for a funkier version of fish and chips.

SERVES 4

450 g (1 lb) skinless cod fillet, cut into small
    chunks

oil, for deep-frying

For the marinade:

½ teaspoon carom seeds

½ teaspoon cumin seeds

½ teaspoon crushed coriander seeds

¼ teaspoon ground turmeric

½ teaspoon dried red chilli flakes

¼ teaspoon tandoori masala powder

½ teaspoon salt

juice of 1 lime

1 garlic clove, sliced very thinly

½ teaspoon natural set low-fat yogurt

1 Combine all the marinade ingredients, to make a smooth paste.

2 Rub the paste into the fish and place in a dish. Cover with clingfilm and leave for 4 hours or overnight.

3 Heat the deep-frying oil to about 170°C or until a cube of bread browns in about 45 seconds and deep-fry the fish, in two or three batches as necessary, until crisp and golden. This will take 7–10 minutes per batch. Remove with a slotted spoon and drain on kitchen paper. Keep warm while you deep-fry the rest.

Dhaniya machchi

(dhun-ee-ya-ma-chi)

CORIANDER FISH

This is a very simple dish, which, with its bright and airy flavours, is lovely to eat in the spring with rice or on a little bed of spaghetti. There is no traditional *tarka* base to this, just a smooth green chilli, garlic and coriander paste that is heated through, to complement the creamy fish.

SERVES 4

2 green chillies, chopped finely

4 garlic cloves, chopped finely

a large handful of chopped fresh coriander

¼ cup oil

1 teaspoon salt

450 g (1 lb) skinless cod fillet, cut into
 large pieces

1 teaspoon tandoori masala powder

fresh coriander sprigs, to garnish

1 Place the chillies, garlic and a large handful of coriander in a blender for a few seconds to mix into a paste.

2 Heat the oil on a low heat in a large saucepan and add the chilli, garlic and coriander mixture.

3 Add the salt and stir well.

4 Add the fish pieces and coat thoroughly.

5 Add ½ cup of water and cover. Cook on a very low heat for 20 minutes.

6 Sprinkle on the tandoori masala.

7 Turn the heat up high to get rid of any excess water. You should be left with a thick sauce. Be careful not to break the fish.

8 Remove from pan with a spatula into a serving dish and pour the sauce over the top. Garnish with coriander sprigs.

COCONUT FISH DREAM

If there is one thing you learn how to make from this book, it should be this sauce. Achingly beautiful to look at and with a taste so dreamy it makes you sigh, this is actually one of the simplest sauces to make. I have coupled it with cod in this recipe but it also works extremely well with small pieces of chicken or with exotic vegetables. The coconut cream adds southern-Indian tones and, along with the butter, makes it truly decadent. With taking only 25 minutes to make, the only danger is you might start treating yourself to this every day.

SERVES 4 – 6

450 g (1 lb) skinless cod fillet, cut into
  large chunks

For the sauce:

1 tablespoon oil

3 teaspoons butter

1 teaspoon cumin seeds

1 onion, grated

1 cup canned chopped tomatoes

1 teaspoon salt

3 green chillies, chopped finely

½ teaspoon red chilli powder

½ teaspoon ground turmeric

a sprinkle of garam masala

1 cup coconut cream

a handful of chopped fresh coriander

1 Heat the oil and butter in a large saucepan with the cumin seeds. When sizzling, add the onion and fry until lightly golden.

2 Turn down the heat. Add the tomatoes, salt, chilli, ground turmeric and chilli powder. Stir well.

3 When shiny and the oil separates, add a sprinkle of garam masala and stir in the coconut cream. Cook gently for 2–3 minutes.

4 Gently add the fish pieces and stir to coat. Cover and cook on a very low heat for 12–15 minutes. Serve sprinkled with a handful of chopped coriander.

Our *Gurudwara* (temple)

GARLICKY PRAWNS

This is an Italian-like baked dish that oozes garlic and cumin flavours. Very simple to prepare, you then just pop it under the grill until bubbling and browned on top. We don't really eat much seafood at home apart from fish and so I was introduced to prawns quite late and my experience was limited to prawn-mayonnaise sandwiches and prawn cocktail. The tomato and chilli sauce accentuates the fleshiness of the prawns and is a delight mopped up with a hot *roti*.

SERVES 2

olive oil

1 teaspoon cumin seeds

4 garlic cloves, sliced very thinly

2 cups peeled, cooked and washed prawns
   (you can use tiger prawns if you wish)

½ cup canned chopped tomatoes, whizzed in
   a blender

1 teaspoon dried red chilli flakes

1 teaspoon salt

1 Heat a little olive oil in a frying pan and add the cumin seeds and garlic.

2 Gently sweat for about 5 minutes – on a very, very low heat – until the garlic is nice and soft. Preheat the grill to hot.

3 Add the prawns to the frying pan and mix thoroughly with the garlic and cumin seeds.

4 Add the tomatoes, chilli and salt and mix well.

5 Transfer to a baking dish and drizzle with more olive oil.

6 Put under the grill until the sauce is slightly browned on top.

SPEEDY TUNA

Cans of tuna are always a good staple to have in the cupboard as they are so versatile. I made this speedy dish of tuna with *tarka*, mushrooms and red onions umpteen times when I was a student and often ate it in toasties, with pasta or on jacket potatoes with a sprinkling of cheese. Remember not to stir or cook the tuna too much or it will just turn to mush; it is best when the chunks still remain intact.

SERVES 2

2 teaspoons oil or butter

½ medium-size red onion, halved again
   lengthways and thinly sliced widthways

1 garlic clove, chopped finely

¼ teaspoon ground turmeric

1 green chilli, chopped finely

a handful of finely chopped fresh coriander

½ teaspoon salt

½ teaspoon garam masala

1 teaspoon tomato purée

3 mushrooms, sliced thinly

2 small cans of tuna in brine, drained

1 Heat the oil or butter and add the onion and garlic. Fry gently for a few minutes until the onion has softened.

2 Add the turmeric, chilli, a handful of coriander, salt, garam masala and tomato purée and stir well. Add a splash of water.

3 Add the mushrooms and stir-fry for a few minutes.

4 Add the tuna and stir well. When tuna is heated through, turn off the heat and serve immediately.

LIP-SMACKING SALMON WRAPPED IN FOIL

Salmon deserves special sauces and you don't get much more special than this. Coaxed with butter, garlic, bay leaves and cinnamon, the salmon pieces are then wrapped and baked with lime slices, coriander leaf and an indulgent scattering of almond shards. This is a very powerfully flavoured dish so you only need a very small amount. It is best served with a delicate dhal, plain *dahi* and lots of *roti* to soak up all the flavours.

SERVES 2

300 g (10½ oz) skinless salmon fillets, cut into
   large chunks

3 tablespoons butter

1 onion, sliced very thinly

3 garlic cloves, chopped very finely

2 fresh tomatoes, diced

1 teaspoon salt

½ teaspoon white sugar

1 teaspoon garam masala

1 teaspoon tandoori masala powder

2 bay leaves

½ teaspoon dried red chilli flakes

1 cinnamon stick

2 lime slices

a handful of chopped fresh coriander

a handful of flaked almonds

1 Preheat the oven to 160°C/fan oven 140°C/Gas Mark 3. Place the salmon on one side of a large sheet of foil on a baking tray.

2 Heat the butter in a saucepan. When melted, add the onion and garlic and gently fry on a very low heat until the onion is softened.

3 Add the tomatoes, salt, sugar, garam masala, tandoori masala, bay leaves, chilli and cinnamon. Cover and continue to cook on a very low heat for 5 minutes.

4 Spoon the mixture over the salmon and top with the lime slices, coriander and almond flakes.

5 Cover with the other side of the sheet of foil, wrapping tightly at the edges. Bake in the oven for 25 minutes.

6 Open the foil and bake for a further 10 minutes.

FISHCAKES WITH BITE

These are a spicy variant of the traditional fishcake, with added crunch from the spring onions and coated in a cheerily colourful coriander-and-gram-flour batter. Serve with thickly cut home-style chips, a dash of light malt vinegar and mushy peas for an alternative chippy-style meal.

MAKES 10 — 12

350 g (12 oz) skinless cod fillet

3 potatoes, peeled and diced

1 teaspoon salt

1 teaspoon garam masala

a squeeze of lemon juice

2 spring onions, chopped finely

3 green chillies, chopped finely

a handful of chopped fresh coriander

For the batter:

1 cup gram flour

a handful of chopped fresh coriander

1 teaspoon salt

oil, for deep-frying

1 Steam the fish for 15 minutes and, when cool enough to handle, flake into a large mixing bowl.

2 Meanwhile, boil the potatoes until tender. Drain and leave to cool.

3 Mix the potatoes into the fish and add the salt, garam masala, lemon juice, spring onions, chillies and a handful of coriander. Mix with a fork and then refrigerate for 1 hour.

4 Make the batter. Mix the gram flour, a handful of coriander and the salt with enough cold water to make a smooth batter.

5 Divide the fish mixture into equal portions and pat into small discs.

6 Heat the deep-frying oil to about 170°C or until a drop of the batter rises to the surface at once. Dip the fishcakes in the batter and then deep-fry them, in two or three batches as necessary, for about 8 minutes or until crisp and golden. Remove with a slotted spoon to kitchen paper to drain and keep warm while you fry the rest.

PAN-FRIED SARDINES WITH YOGURT

I find sardines so utterly boring except when cooked fresh on a barbecue on holiday or when they are cooked like this. I make this dish quite often for supper, as I love the way the flavours melt together in the pan with the olive oil. Seasoned with chilli and ground coriander, the lemon slices, garlic, fresh tomato and onion provide a stunning backdrop for the sardines, which are added and cooked until crisp and golden. Sometimes I also add cooked potato slices for a more substantial all-in-one meal. I then pour it all into a dish and top with a good amount of *dahi*.

SERVES 2

2 tablespoons oil (I like to use olive oil for this)

2 teaspoons ground coriander

1 teaspoon salt

½ teaspoon red chilli powder

1 garlic clove, sliced very thinly

3 lemon slices

1 fresh tomato, diced

¼ medium onion, sliced thinly

2 x 120 g cans of sardines in brine, drained

a handful of chopped fresh coriander

natural set low-fat yogurt, to serve

1 Heat the oil in a pan and add all the ingredients except the sardines and fresh coriander. Fry gently until the onions are softened.

2 Add the sardines, placing them evenly and directly on to the pan surface. Brown on one side and then turn over.

3 Sprinkle a little chopped coriander on each serving and add a dollop of yogurt.

Different generations of British Asian society

chaul *(chorl)*

RICE

PERFECT, FLUFFY WHITE RICE

A lot of people are confused as to why their rice doesn't turn out the way it should. I read reader's queries in magazines and listen to phone-ins on cookery shows and it is always the same complaint: either the rice clumps together or it becomes sticky. Perfectly cooked basmati rice with pearly, smooth singular grains is very easy to achieve. Firstly, you must always wash the rice before cooking until the water runs clear, as this eliminates the starchiness that causes the stickiness. With regards to clumping, treat cooked rice gently. Never, ever stir or plunge a spoon straight into cooked rice to take a portion. Before serving, always take a fork and lightly graze the surface of the rice to loosen the grains. Work your way through the pan, shaking off any rice that sticks to the fork, so that you have singular grains. Only then should you very gently use a spoon or spatula to take a portion and place on a plate.

SERVES 2

1 cup basmati rice   **a tiny knob of butter**

1 Rinse the rice in a saucepan; to do this place the rice in a saucepan and fill with cold water. Pour the water away and fill again. Keep on until the water runs clear.

2 Add 2 cups of cold water to the rice and stir. Place on a medium heat and add the knob of butter, do not stir. Bring to the boil. Stir

3 Turn the heat down low, cover and simmer for about 10 minutes until all the water has been absorbed. Check by tilting the pan to the side to see if there is any water left.

4 Turn the heat off. Using the tip of a fork, gently loosen the rice, working your way through the pan. If you are heavy handed the rice will break and go mushy. Loosen each grain gently.

5 Gently transfer to a serving dish.

WILD RICE WITH CASHEWS

You can buy packets of wild rice mixed with basmati rice in the supermarkets quite easily. I love the visual contrast of the long rough black grains against the angelic polished white grains. The texture is also a wonderful combination; the basmati rice is soft with its milky taste whilst the wild rice adds a natural texture and a nutty taste. Combined with cashew nuts and cardamom pods, this rice has quite a Mughal court feel to it and goes well with aromatic lamb dishes.

SERVES 2

1 teaspoon oil

3 green cardamom pods

¼ cup halved unsalted cashews

1 cup wild rice mixed with basmati rice, washed

1   Heat the oil in a saucepan and add the cardamoms and cashews. Gently fry for 3–4 minutes.

2   Add the rice and stir-fry for 2 minutes.

3   Add 2 cups of cold water and stir well. Bring to the boil.

4   Reduce the heat to low and cover. Simmer for 10–12 minutes until the water has all been absorbed.

5   Loosen with a fork gently and transfer to a serving dish.

RICE WITH ONION, PEAS AND CUMIN

This rice, although eaten with a variety of dishes, goes hand in hand with *khadhi* (page 190) to form my most favourite meal. When I was at uni, I really missed this rice and attempted to make it from what I could remember. However, I got it all a bit upside-down and back to front and boiled the rice first and then attempted to stir-fry it with the cumin, onions and peas. Needless to say, I ended up with a sticky, gooey mess with raw cumin seeds poking out, and had to order pizza. When my Mum showed me how to make it properly, I felt like a real dunce. So here it is for all of you, the way my Mum makes it so that you can enjoy it in all its glory.

SERVES 4

1 tablespoon oil

1 teaspoon cumin seeds

½ onion, halved again lengthways and then thinly sliced widthways

1 teaspoon salt

2 cups frozen peas

2 cups basmati rice, washed

1 Heat the oil and the cumin seeds in a saucepan. When the cumin seeds are sizzling, add the onion and salt. Fry on a gentle heat until the onions are softened and translucent and the brown colour of the cumin seeds has rubbed off on to the onions.

2 Add the peas and stir well. Add the rice. Turn the heat up and stir-fry for 2 minutes.

3 Add 2¾ cups of cold water and bring to the boil.

4 Stir well. Reduce the heat to low, partly cover and simmer for 15–20 minutes, until all the water has evaporated.

5 Loosen with a fork gently and transfer to a serving dish.

CHILLI, LIME AND CORIANDER RICE

This is very simple as there is no frying stage. Simply pop it all in the pan and wait for it to cook. The colour of the chillies and coriander leaf make it vibrant and the lime perks it up a little. I made this at a dinner party while one of my guests watched – she couldn't believe something so delicious could be so simple to make. Serve with chicken dishes or kebabs and chutneys.

SERVES 4

2 cups basmati rice, washed

a small knob of butter

2 red chillies, chopped finely

a handful of chopped fresh coriander

juice of 1 lime

1 Place the rice in a large saucepan and add 4 cups/1 litre/1¾ pints of cold water.

2 Add the butter, chillies, coriander and lime and stir well.

3 Bring to the boil.

4 Reduce the heat to low, cover and simmer for 20 minutes or until all the water has evaporated.

5 Loosen with a fork gently and transfer to a serving dish.

JEWELLED RICE FIT FOR A RANI

This is what you make when you are having a party and you want your guests to be fascinated by your culinary talents. I spent years wondering how on earth this was made. Some of the grains of rice are white, some green, some red and some yellow, all separately. I could not understand how these were cooked in the same pan without the colours mixing together. The secret is actually very easy and has erased all the mystery – always use powdered, never liquid, food colouring and steam gently with kitchen paper in-between the lid and the pan. Add some butter, cloves and cardamom and you have magically fragrant, multicoloured rice. When the chopped green pistachios are sprinkled over the top you are left with what looks like a plate of royal jewels.

SERVES 2 – 4

1½ cups basmati rice, washed

1 teaspoon butter

5 cloves

6 green cardamom pods, split

green, red and yellow food colour powder

¼ cup chopped pistachios

1 Leave the rice to soak in water. Meanwhile, fill a large saucepan to three-quarters full with cold water and bring to the boil.

2 Drain the rice and add to the pan. Simmer for 10 minutes.

3 Drain the rice into a colander immediately.

4 Heat the butter in a large pan on a very low heat. Add the cloves and cardamom. Stir well and add the rice. Using a palette knife or a spatula, gently push the rice from one side of the pan to the other until all liquid has dried off but the rice is still moist. Be very careful not to break the rice grains.

5 Sprinkle dots of the three food colourings on to the rice, making sure the colours do not touch each other. Leave some white rice spaces.

6 Place three sheets of kitchen paper (one on top of the other to make it thicker) over the pan and place the lid on top.

7 Keeping the heat very, very low, leave to steam for 15 minutes.

8 Turn off the heat, gently loosen with a fork and transfer to a serving dish. Sprinkle with the pistachios.

SAFFRON, ALMOND AND CRACKED BLACK PEPPER RICE

Saffron is, as everyone knows, the most expensive spice in the world and it gives a unique flavour and golden colour to dishes with only a few strands. Some people use turmeric as a cheaper alternative to turn rice yellow but that leaves a very bitter taste. Food colouring, in comparison, tends to give a slightly sweet flavour. Saffron is really the only way to strike the right balance for a savoury taste. The cracked black peppercorns lend muskiness whilst the almonds add creaminess. This rice is great with any meat or fish dishes and looks great presented with a few whole almonds on top.

SERVES 2

2 teaspoons oil

a handful of flaked almonds

salt

a few saffron strands

1 teaspoon black peppercorns, cracked in a pestle and mortar

1 cup basmati rice, washed

1 Heat the oil in a saucepan and gently fry the almonds, a sprinkle of salt, peppercorns and saffron for a few minutes.
2 Add the rice and stir-fry for 3–4 minutes.
3 Add 2 cups of cold water and stir well. Bring to the boil.
4 Reduce the heat to low, cover and simmer for 20 minutes.
5 Loosen with a fork gently and transfer to a serving dish.

SPECIAL MIXED VEGETABLE RICE

It is always a good idea to keep a bag of diced mixed vegetables in the freezer as they can be used in so many ways. This colourful rice is pretty much always served to guests (I suppose it is our version of special fried rice) as it shows you have gone to a bit of effort. You can use any vegetables you wish but peppers, sweetcorn, carrots and peas are favourites. It is usually served with a meat and vegetarian dish and sometimes also a dhal.

SERVES 6

¾ cup oil

1 onion, halved lengthways, halved again
   lengthways and then thinly sliced widthways

½ cup frozen diced mixed vegetables

1 teaspoon cumin seeds

2 teaspoons salt

2 cups basmati rice, washed

1 Heat the oil in a large wok and add the onion. When the onion is slightly golden, add the vegetables.

2 Fry for 1 minute and then add the cumin seeds. Fry for another minute and add the salt.

3 Add 3 cups of cold water, cover and bring to the boil.

4 When boiling, add the rice to the pan. Use a spoon to edge the rice in to make sure it is covered with the water but do not stir. Leave uncovered until boiling.

5 Reduce the heat to very, very low, so that it is almost off, cover and cook for 20 minutes.

6 Loosen with a fork gently and transfer to a serving dish.

BUTTER-FRIED RICE

My Mum often eats this on Sunday afternoons, with sausages, baked beans and *achaar*. It sounds an odd combination but makes a hearty meal. She told me that when she was young, that would be the Saturday night meal in the house, as her Dad really loved it. He loved the British food he discovered when he came to this country and always adapted it. Unfortunately, I never knew my Granddad, he died before I was born, but this rice is just like all the ways people describe him – fun, warm and uncomplicated. So this recipe is in his memory.

SERVES 1

2 tablespoons butter

½ teaspoon salt

½ teaspoon garam masala

½ cup basmati rice, cooked (page 146)

1 Heat the butter and add the salt and garam masala.
2 Add the rice and stir-fry until fully heated. Transfer to a serving dish. Serve at once.

Me and *Pooiji* (aunt)

SPICY RICE

This is my Indian version of a sort of risotto and is lovely comfort food. I usually eat it in bed whilst watching old black and white Audrey Hepburn movies. The coconut cream subdues the chilli and the sweetcorn adds little flecks of creamy sunshine. It is even better reheated the next day.

SERVES 2

1 tablespoon oil

1 teaspoon dried red chilli flakes

1 green chilli, chopped finely

1 teaspoon salt

½ cup sweetcorn kernels

¼ cup coconut cream

1 cup basmati rice, cooked (page 146)

chopped fresh coriander

1 Heat the oil in a large frying pan and add the chilli flakes, chilli and salt. Fry for 1 minute and then add the sweetcorn.

2 Fry for a further minute and add the coconut cream. Cook for 1 further minute and add the rice.

3 Stir-fry for 3–4 minutes until the rice is thoroughly heated.

4 Sprinkle with a handful of chopped coriander

SIMPLE VEGETABLE BIRYANI

The biryanis I have come across in restaurants are completely different to the home-made versions made by my friends' parents that I have had the pleasure of sampling. Biryani is a very special Mughal dish and does not really have multicoloured sweetish rice or an insipid yellow sauce. It is made with whole spices and the rice is layered with vegetables or meat in a thick sauce and then baked in the oven. This is a very simple version to try. Make sure to fry the onions until quite dark brown and serve carefully, to preserve the beautiful layers.

SERVES 4 — 6

2 cups basmati rice, washed	1 cup natural set low-fat yogurt
6 tablespoons oil	1 cup canned chopped tomatoes
1 onion, sliced thinly	1 teaspoon cumin seeds
2 garlic cloves, chopped finely	1 stick cassia bark
1 teaspoon grated fresh root ginger	1 tablespoon black peppercorns
1 teaspoon salt	1 teaspoon ground coriander
2 green chillies, chopped finely	450 g (1 lb) frozen diced mixed vegetables
1 teaspoon garam masala	chopped fresh coriander

1 Preheat the oven to 170°C/fan oven 150°C/Gas Mark 3. Cook the rice as described on page 146 for 10 minutes, leaving it still slightly underdone. Drain off the remaining water and leave aside.

2 Heat the oil in a large frying pan and fry the onion until brown and slightly singed at the edges.

3 Add the garlic, ginger, salt, chillies, garam masala, yogurt, tomatoes, cumin seeds, cassia, peppercorns and ground coriander. Stir and cook on a low heat until shiny and the oil separates. Add the vegetables and stir-fry for 5 minutes.

4 Place a layer of rice in a large ovenproof dish. Add a layer of the vegetable mixture. Add another layer of rice and another layer of the vegetable mixture and so on until the last layer of rice is placed on top.

5 Cook in the oven for 20 minutes.

6 Gently loosen the very top layer with a fork. Use a spatula to cut portions of the rice so that the layers remain intact. Sprinkle with a handful of the coriander and serve.

roti

(roh-tee)

BREADS

ROTI

I don't know a single Indian person who uses the word 'chapatti'. Most people call this bread *roti* at home. I suppose the technical term for this particular recipe is *phulke* as the method includes the stage where the *roti* is puffed up on the open flame. (Traditionally, *phulke* refers to large, thin *roti* made in *Gurudwaras* for *Langar* in India, which are always puffed up on a naked flame.) Some people don't do this stage and simply pat with a tea towel but that is not the way my family and I make them. Of all the items an Indian girl learns how to make, these are the hardest to master. Getting them perfectly round, all the same size, with just enough brown spots, puffed up and evenly cooked, and yet still soft takes years of practice.

Until recently, girls were still expected to use their bare hands in the flames to turn them over but now people are cottoning on a little to fire hazard issues. Therefore, although the use of *chimta* (tongs) is sometimes frowned upon as being a wimpy cop-out, it is slowly being accepted. In any case, this can only be done if you have a gas hob; otherwise, lightly press each side of the *roti* on the *thawa* with a clean tea towel to puff them up gently. When you see light brown spots, the *roti* is cooked. *Rotia* are best eaten immediately but they can be wrapped in foil to keep warm for a short while.

These took me years to learn and I discovered that the secret is all in the timing. Therefore I have tried to be as precise as possible with this recipe. Have fun practising!

MAKES 6

2 cups roti flour, white, brown or wholemeal   **a little butter**

My Mum cooking *roti* on the *thawa*

1 Place the flour in a large, shallow mixing bowl. Using hands, add water very slowly to bind the flour together. Wash your hands.

2 Knead the dough thoroughly using your knuckles, folding the dough in and turning over repeatedly. Cover and refrigerate for 30 minutes minimum.

3 Rinse the *thawa* and place on a low heat. Take a large shallow dish, fill with *roti* flour and place on the worktop. Get a rolling pin, a plate, a pair of tongs, some butter and a teaspoon.

4 Take the dough and divide into equal portions. Each portion should be the size of a small satsuma.

5 Dust the worktop lightly with some of the flour from the dish. Take a portion of the dough and roll into an even ball in your hands. Place the ball on the work surface and flatten with your fingers. Cup your hands and use the edges of your hands (your little finger side) to make the disc perfectly round. Flatten again with your fingers.

6 Take a rolling pin and gently roll out to form a flat round. Turn over and roll the other side.

7 Lay in the dish of flour to coat, turn over and do the same with the other side. Shake off excess flour and lay the *roti* on the worktop again. Roll out, using a circular motion to increase the size of the *roti*, and then turn over and roll the other side. Continue this process until you have an even and round *roti* the size of a tea plate. It should not be too thin.

8 Gently pick up the *roti* and gently toss from palm to palm in a pat-a-cake action, rotating the *roti* to shake off excess flour and even out the size. Slap flat on to the centre of the *thawa*. After 4 seconds, when you see the *roti* becoming slightly brown, turn over with the tongs. When small bubbles begin to appear, about 6 seconds, pick up the *roti* with the tongs with one hand whilst picking up the *thawa* away from the heat with the other.

9 Place the *roti*, same-side down, straight on to the gas ring, moving around slightly with the tongs. The *roti* should completely puff up. Turn over immediately for 2 seconds and then return the *thawa* to the ring.

10 Place the *roti*, most-cooked-side upwards, on a plate and spread with a little butter using the teaspoon.

Plain parathe

(pa-rort-he)

LIGHLY FRIED BREAD

This bread is made with the same flour as normal *roti* but has a layer of butter in the middle and is then lightly fried in more butter to make it golden, crisp and flaky. *Parathe* are usually eaten for breakfast at weekends or for picnics. In my family, no trip to Alton Towers or the seaside was complete without a good batch of *parathe* lurking in the boot. And they are often wrapped in foil and given to students to eat on the train or coach back to university. It is best to use ghee when making these, as butter tends to smoke, but some people do not like the taste of ghee. My Mum sometimes uses very mild olive oil for a healthier version.

MAKES ABOUT 4

2 cups roti flour   **butter, ghee or oil**

1 Make up the dough as for *roti* (page 158).

2 Rinse the *thawa* and place on a very low heat. Get a shallow dish and fill with *roti* flour, get a fish slice, a large plate, a rolling pin, a knife and a teaspoon.

3 Take a portion larger than that for a *roti*, a little larger than a satsuma , and roll into a ball in your hands.

4 Dust the work surface with some of the flour and, using the same method as *roti*, roll out the disc. Roll it out larger than a *roti*, to the size of a large plate.

5 Using a knife, spread a little butter on the centre of the *roti*.

6 Fold the top of the *paratha* down to the middle and press flat so the top is now straight. Fold the bottom side in so the curved edge meets the now straight edge of the top. You should have a long horizontal rectangle with curved edges. Fold the right hand side into the middle. Fold the left side in so that the left hand edge meets the far right hand edge. You should now have a square.

7 Dip the square in the flour, making sure that the edges, where the butter could ooze out, are covered in flour too.

8 Gently roll out the square, dipping in flour as you go, to the size of a square slightly smaller than the size of a dinner plate. It should not be too thin.

9 Place on the centre of the *thawa*. After 10 seconds, using the fish slice, flip over. Smear the side facing you with butter, ghee or oil.

10 Flip over to the other side; smear that side with butter, ghee or oil too. Flip over again and cook till golden and crisp.

Langar

This is the meal provided at the Gurudwara (the Sikh temple) and forms one of the ways in which Sikhs may carry out their duty to work and provide for the whole human family (other ways include cleaning the Gurudwara or helping with a community project, for example). Devotees can pay for expenses, bring provisions, help cook and wash dishes to help contribute to the Langar that is offered daily, and free, at the Gurudwara to all who enter. The Devotees sit down together in a row on the floor – known as Pangat – and enjoy the simple food offered on thalis (stainless-steel trays with little individual compartments for each dish). All share equally and no one will be refused. The meal is vegetarian and consists of roti (known as phulke in the Gurudwara), dhal, sabjia, dahi and achaar with tea or water.

Makhi di roti

(ma-khee-dee-roh-tee)

CORN FLOUR BREAD

To make these in the really traditional way is very difficult. My **Pooiji** can do it, making the **roti** in mid-air with just her hands, but even she says she can only do it because she has had 40 years to practice. The more common method, which is still pretty difficult but manageable, is to make them flat on a board. Making the dough takes practice too as it requires kneading with boiling water. The result, though, is worth all the effort 10 times over.

MAKES 4

1 cup fine corn flour

1 cup coarse corn flour

a little butter

1   Boil a kettle of water. Place the 2 cups of corn flour in a bowl and mix together with hands. Transfer to a larger shallow mixing bowl.

2   Very carefully, add tiny amounts of boiling water bit by bit to the flour and mix with a fork until you have gathered all the flour together to form a single mass. Using hands, knead the dough thoroughly, pressing in with your knuckles, adding more boiling water as you go along. The dough must be firm.

3   Rinse the *thawa* and put it on a very low heat. Place some fine corn flour in a shallow dish. Put some boiling water in a small bowl.

4   Sprinkle a small round wooden chopping board with some of the flour.

5   Dip your hand in the flour and then break off some of the dough – the amount should be slightly larger than a satsuma.

6   Roll in your hands; it should be completely smooth with no cracks.

7   Flatten it into a disc in the palm of your hands and pat with some more boiling water to keep it from drying and cracking – it must be kept supple.

8   Place the disc on the chopping board and, using the palm of your hand, press down on it and rotate it to enlarge it to the size of a tea plate. If you feel you can't push it out any more without breaking it, add more flour.

9   Use boiling water to seal any cracks around the edges.

10   Gently place in the centre of the *thawa*. Leave for 15 seconds and turn over.

11   Cook for another 10 seconds and remove. You should have a *roti* that has one side with dark brown spots.

12   Coat with some butter on the side with the spots.

STUFFED PARATHE

Stuffed *parathe* (the plural of *paratha*) are the Indian equivalent of the Great British Sunday Fry Up Breakfast. Sundays are simply not the same without these delicious breads, most people can wolf down two without even realising. They are usually served to guests who have stayed over and everyone loves them. Mum in Nottingham (actually my Nan – for some reason we have always called her 'Mum', which can get a little confusing) makes the best *aloo parathe* ever. She makes them with a thick layer of the potato mixture whilst keeping the *roti* on either side delicately crisp. They are so substantial that she sometimes serves them as the main meal in the evening. My *David Mamma* (uncle) showed me a trick on how to eat them with *dahi* when I was about 12. Instead of dipping each piece into a separate bowlful of *dahi*, you carefully peel back the top *roti*, spread the yogurt on the hot *aloo* mixture and replace the *roti*. Then add a little lump of butter on the hot *paratha*. The butter melts on the top and as you break each piece, the yogurt oozes through. Messy, but thoroughly delicious. I recently enjoyed a holiday in Turkey with my family and we discovered that, in the villages, the women make a Turkish pancake that is very similar to the stuffed *paratha*. Their flour is different and the pancakes are thinner but the potato version is very similar and is spiced with the same ingredients. I ate so many that my Dad said I was going to turn into a Turkish pancake. I have included some typical filling recipes here but feel free to experiment.

MAKES ABOUT 8 – 10

parathe dough, made with 10 cups of roti flour (page 26)

butter, ghee or oil

For Mum in Nottingham's aloo parathe:

4 potatoes, peeled, diced and boiled

½ onion, grated and squeezed of all water

a handful of chopped fresh coriander

2 teaspoons garam masala

1½ teaspoons salt

1 green chilli, chopped finely

For special-mix parathe:

4 potatoes, peeled diced and boiled

½ onion, grated and squeezed of all water

3 spring onions, chopped very finely

8 mushrooms, chopped very finely

2 tomatoes, de-seeded and chopped very finely

2 teaspoons garam masala

1½ teaspoons salt

½ teaspoon red chilli powder

For mooliwala parathe:

1 mooli, peeled and grated and squeezed of all water

½ onion, grated and squeezed of all water

2 teaspoons garam masala

1½ teaspoons salt

1 green chilli, chopped finely

a handful of finely chopped fresh coriander

1 green chilli, chopped finely

For keema parathe:

2 teaspoons garam masala

4 cups of lamb mince, fried with a little oil

1½ teaspoons salt

1 Combine all the ingredients for the filling you wish to have in a large mixing bowl with a fork. Refrigerate for at least 30 minutes.

2 Meanwhile, prepare the dough as for *roti* (page 158), using 10 cups of flour. Refrigerate for at least 30 minutes.

3 Rinse the *thawa* and place on a very low heat.

4 Get a shallow dish and fill with *roti* flour, get a fish slice, a large plate, a rolling pin, a knife and a teaspoon.

5 Take a portion larger than that for a *roti*, a little larger than a satsuma, and roll into a ball in your hands.

6 Dust the work surface with some of the flour and, using the same method as with *roti*, roll out the disc. Roll it out larger than a *roti*, to the size of a large plate.

7 Put aside and roll out another ball to exactly the same size.

8 Using a fork, add a thin layer of the stuffing mixture to the *roti*, using to fork to make sure it is an even layer and reaches almost to the edges.

9 Carefully place the other *roti* on top using the palm of your hand to smooth it on to make sure there are no creases. Use fingers to seal the edges.

10 Carefully place the *paratha* on the centre of the *thawa*. Leave to cook for 15 seconds.

11 Using a fish slice, gently turn it over and smear with butter, ghee or oil. Leave for 10 seconds and turn over. Smear with butter, ghee or oil. Keep cooking and turning till golden and brown.

A *thawa*

Dhalwale parathe

(dhaal-vaale-pa-rort-he)
LENTIL PARATHE

You know how English people make leftovers into a hotpot or stew? Well we pack them all into a *paratha*. This variation has a dough made from flour, spices, chillies, onion and any leftover dhal or even leftover *sabji*. My *Chachiji* likes to add a little grated cheese whilst my Mum throws in a good a handful of fenugreek leaves. You just combine it all and then roll it all out ready to fry lightly on the *thawa* like a plain *paratha*. All you need is a little *achaar* and a large glass of *lassi* for a wonderful filling brunch.

MAKES ABOUT 6

2 cups roti flour	**1½ teaspoons garam masala**
½ onion, grated and squeezed of all water	**a good handful of chopped fresh coriander**
⅓ + ¼ cup of cooked dhal	**2 green chillies, chopped finely**
1½ teaspoons salt	**butter, ghee or oil**

1 Place all the ingredients, except the butter, ghee or oil, in a large mixing bowl and mix well with a spoon.

2 Make the dough in the same way as *roti* dough (page 158).

3 Rinse the *thawa* and place on a very low heat.

4 Get a shallow dish and fill with *roti* flour, get a fish slice, a large plate, a rolling pin, a knife and some butter, ghee or oil with a teaspoon.

5 Cook in the same way as plain *parathe* (page 160).

Leicester naniji's methi roti

(me-thee-roh-tee)

FENUGREEK LEAF BREAD

Leicester **Naniji** is my Mum's best-friend-since-childhood's Mum and so she is like a second Nan to me too. **Naniji** and her husband were best friends with my Nan and Granddad and used to hang out back in the old days when they owned a social club in Nottingham. She is about 70 and yet is ridiculously beautiful, is very witty and always makes me lovely food whenever we visit (which we often combine with a lot of Indian clothes shopping!). The last time we went to visit, she made these delicious fenugreek, gram flour and ginger **rotia** for lunch before we hit the shops. I liked them so much that I had three whilst my Mum had one (which is the normal amount). I could hardly get up after that.

MAKES 10 — 12

2 cups roti flour

1 cup gram flour

2 tablespoons grated fresh root ginger (not frozen)

1½ teaspoons salt

2 teaspoons garam masala

2 green chillies, chopped finely

3 generous handfuls of chopped fresh fenugreek leaves

butter, ghee or oil

1 Combine all the ingredients in a large mixing bowl with a spoon.

2 Make the dough in the same way as *roti* dough (page 158).

3 Take a portion larger than that for a *roti*, a little larger than a satsuma, and roll into a ball with your hands.

4 Dust the work surface with some of the flour and, using the same method as for making *roti*, roll out the disc. Roll it out larger than a *roti*, to the size of a large plate.

5 Place on the centre of the *thawa*. Wait for 15 seconds and then flip over.

6 Smear with butter, ghee or oil. After 10 seconds flip over and smear the other side with butter, ghee or oil. Cook until crisp and golden.

Pooria

(poo-hree-a)
DEEP-FRIED BREAD

A must for any party, these are often made with the evening meal at a birthday party or Christmas party family get-together. They are deep-fried until puffed up and golden and are wonderfully crispy. Just the thing to have with any chicken dish, mixed vegetable rice, dhal and palhe (page 181) before collapsing and watching an Indian film on video together. You can also serve these topped with a little Maharajah's Mash (page 85), palhe, sukke chole (page 68), imli chutney (page 179), grated raw onion and a little sev to make a quick and delicious chaat.

MAKES ABOUT 8

2 cups roti flour   **oil, for deep-frying**

1 Make the dough in exactly the same way as for *roti* (page 158).

2 Using the same principles as *roti*, but using smaller balls, roll out smaller *rotis* to the size of saucers. Make them slightly thicker than *roti*.

3 Heat the oil to about 170°C or until a little piece of the dough rises to the surface at once. Deep-fry the *pooria* until they are puffed up and brown. Drain on kitchen paper.

Bhature

(pah-too-re)

MILKY BREAD

Now this is a special *roti*. These are either made for a very special dinner party or are served with the meal at wedding receptions. It is a shame that now the trend is for easier pre-packed naan bread cut into slices to be served. I'll have no such thing at my wedding, I can tell you. They are made with yogurt and milk to form a creamy dough and are then deep-fried. The result is a soft, cloud-like bread that is delicious with *sukke chole* (page 68) and other full-flavoured dishes.

MAKES 4

1 cup self-raising flour

a pinch of salt

2 tablespoons natural set low-fat yogurt

full-fat milk

oil, for deep-frying

1 Mix the flour, salt and yogurt in a large mixing bowl with your hands. Add enough milk to form a dough – add drop by drop.

2 Knead to a firm dough.

3 Cover and refrigerate for 15 minutes.

4 Roll out to small discs the size of saucers – do not make them too thin. Use self-raising flour to dust the work surface and to dip them in.

5 Heat the oil to about 170°C or until a little piece of the dough rises to the surface at once. Deep-fry the *bhature*, turning over with a perforated spoon, until golden, puffed up and soft. Drain on kitchen paper.

MUM'S ORIGINAL ROTI

My Mum actually invented these one day after accidentally using plain flour instead of self-raising flour to make *bhature*. They turned out to be a delicious variation of deep-fried bread and I think they should be made more often.

MAKES 4

1 cup plain flour

a pinch of salt

2 tablespoons natural set low-fat yogurt

full-fat milk

oil, for deep-frying

1   Mix the flour, salt and yogurt in a large mixing bowl with your hands. Add enough milk to form a dough – add it drop by drop.

2   Knead to a firm dough.

3   Cover and refrigerate for 15 minutes.

4   Roll out to small discs the size of saucers – do not make them too thin. Use plain flour to dust the surface and to dip them in.

5   Heat the oil to about 170°C, or when a little piece of dough rises to the surface at once. Deep-fry the discs, turning over with a perforated spoon, until puffed up, crisp and golden.

A Punjabi drummer sign outside the infamous Glassy Junction pub in Southall

nal nal

chalna

(naal-naal-chuhl-naa) **ACCOMPANIMENTS**

TOMATO AND ONION CHUTNEY

I have been making this for years, not only as a chutney for Indian dishes but also to pep up English food. Make sure it has a coarse consistency. It is a spicy variant of fresh tomato salsa and is great in fajitas, with nachos and in toasted cheese sandwiches.

¼ onion

¼ red onion

2 spring onions

4 green chillies

a large handful of chopped fresh coriander

a dash of light malt vinegar

a dash of lemon juice

½ teaspoon salt

¼ teaspoon sugar

a dash of tomato ketchup

2 tomatoes, chopped

½ teaspoon garam masala

1 Whizz all the ingredients in a blender.

2 Refrigerate for 30 minutes before serving.

MASALA KETCHUP

You'll find a bottle of ketchup in every British-Asian household as we have really taken it to our hearts. This variant adds a little extra *desi* vibe to it, with a little crushed roasted cumin and garam masala. Great on *Masala* Burgers or Very Hot Dogs (pages 131 and 130).

1 teaspoon oil

1 teaspoon cumin seeds

1 teaspoon garam masala

½ cup tomato ketchup

1 Heat the oil and fry the cumin seeds until sizzling. Turn off the heat and stir in the garam masala.

2 Leave to cool and then stir into the ketchup.

MASALA AND VINEGAR RUB FOR MEAT

I used to rub this into defrosted frozen beef burgers when I was a kid, to add a little extra taste. Rubbed into raw meats that are then left to marinate for a couple of hours, it gives a tangy quality when the meat is grilled or barbecued.

2 tablespoons light malt vinegar

2 tablespoons tomato ketchup

1 teaspoon garam masala

1 teaspoon ground coriander

1 garlic clove, crushed

1 Mix the ingredients well in a bowl.

2 Use to rub into meat as a marinade before grilling or barbecuing.

Tharwala dahi

(thuhr-vaa-laa-da-hee)

CUCUMBER YOGHURT

My Dad often treats me to this when I come home on a Friday evening. When I see this in a bowl sitting on the worktop I know that he has made a delicious meat dish with fragrant rice and my stomach starts rumbling. I love the flavour of the cucumber with the yogurt offset by the chilli. I also like piling this on to a jacket potato for a healthy topping.

¾ x 500 g carton of natural set low-fat yogurt

milk

¼ cucumber, peeled, grated and squeezed of water

¼ onion, grated and squeezed of water

1 green chilli, chopped finely

½ teaspoon salt

1 teaspoon garam masala

½ teaspoon red chilli powder

fresh coriander sprigs, to garnish

1 Mix the yogurt with enough water to make a runny yogurt – the cucumber will thicken it so make it quite runny.

2 Add the cucumber, onion, chilli and salt and stir well.

3 Decorate with the garam masala, chilli powder and sprigs of coriander.

TEN-SECOND YOGURT AND MINT CHUTNEY

This is a delicious pale-yellow, mild, minty chutney that literally takes seconds to make as all you do is stir the ingredients together. It goes perfectly with kebabs, fried fish, *samose*, *pakore* and other snacks. It looks very authentic served in little bowls but little do people know how quickly you knocked it together!

1 cup natural set low-fat yogurt	**¼ teaspoon salt**
milk	**¼ teaspoon garam masala**
¼ teaspoon ground turmeric	**2 teaspoons mint sauce**

1 Combine the yogurt with enough milk to make quite a runny mixture
2 Add the rest of the ingredients and stir well.

CHUTNEY FOR GUESTS

A sharp and juicy chutney that is whizzed up in no time at all and goes well with Pooiji's Original Fritters (page 63). This forest-green accompaniment is just the thing to serve to guests when you want to make an impression.

½ bunch of fresh coriander

8 green chillies

7 teaspoons lemon juice

2 teaspoons sugar

3 spring onions

1 Whizz all the ingredients in a blender and serve.

Imli chutney

(im-il-ee)

TAMARIND CHUTNEY

It has been my job to make this gorgeous sweet and sour *imli* chutney for as long as I can remember (I never minded as it would get me out of making the harder things!). But my connections to it go much further back than that. My Mum told me that she used to crave this when pregnant with me and that sometimes she would even eat pieces of tamarind torn right off the block. This is mouth-watering served with *samose*, *pakore* and other snacks.

½ x 200 g (7 oz) block of tamarind

3 teaspoons garam masala

3 teaspoons salt

5 teaspoons sugar

4 tablespoons tomato ketchup

a dash of lemon juice

2 green chillies, chopped finely

½ medium-size onion, sliced very finely

2 carrots, peeled and grated

2 spring onions, chopped finely

a handful of chopped fresh coriander

1 Place the tamarind in a saucepan or bowl, cover with boiling water and leave to soak for 10 minutes.

2 Using a spoon, break the tamarind up and stir thoroughly to combine as much as possible with the water.

3 Strain the liquid through a tea strainer into a large mixing bowl.

4 Add a little more boiling water to the solids that have remained. Use a spoon again to try and dissolve them into the water. Strain again into the bowl.

5 Repeat this process until little solids remain.

6 Try and push these solids through the strainer by pouring on more boiling water and squeezing with the teaspoon.

7 Discard any final remaining solids when you have pushed through as much as you can.

8 Stir the liquid thoroughly.

9 Add the remaining ingredients and stir well.

10 Refrigerate for at least 30 minutes.

Mammiji (aunt, centre) and relatives at the *Gurudwara* (temple)

Bhoondiwala dahi

(bhoon-dee-vaa-laa-da-hee)

GRAM FLOUR BALLS IN YOGURT

Tiny little balls of deep-fried gram flour – *bhoondi* – are cooled, soaked, squeezed and then added to yogurt to make this very traditional accompaniment. I love it when I go to the *Gurudwara* and eat simple dhal, *roti* and this *dahi*. No matter how we make it at home it somehow never tastes as good as it does as part of the *Langar* (the meal made and served at the *Gurudwara*).

For the bhoondi:

1 cup gram flour

salt

oil, for deep-frying

To serve:

¾ x 500 g carton natural set low-fat yogurt

milk

½ teaspoon of salt

½ teaspoon garam masala

a handful of chopped fresh coriander

1 Place the gram flour and a pinch of salt in a large bowl.

2 Add enough cold water to make a smooth paste – not too thick and not too runny. It needs to be able to drop quickly through a perforated spoon.

3 Place a clean, large perforated metal spoon over enough oil to deep-fry, heated to about 170°C or when a drop of the gram-flour batter rises to the surface at once.

4 Slowly pour the mixture through the spoon and into the oil.

5 Fry for around 3 minutes and then use a clean perforated spoon to lift the *bhoondi* out.

6 Drain on kitchen paper and leave to cool for a few hours.

7 When they have thoroughly cooled, place in a large bowl of boiling water for 5 minutes.

8 Squeeze out all the water from them and put aside on a plate.

9 Mix the yogurt with enough milk to make a runny mixture.

10 Add the *bhoondi*, salt and garam masala and stir well. Serve scattered with a handful of chopped coriander.

Palhe made from scratch

(pal-he)

LENTIL BALLS IN YOGURT

Also one of my favourites (I have a lot of favourite foods, don't I?), this is usually made at parties or when you are holding a special dinner party. You can get ready made mixes for these but there is nothing like the real McCoy. They are balls of crushed lentils with ginger and cumin that are deep-fried, cooled, squeezed and added to yogurt for an accompaniment which is in a league of its own. These were served at my cousin Jasneal's *Akhand Path* recently and, as I moved along the counter with my tray, my *Choti Pooiji* made sure she gave me two, saying 'I know you like your *palhe*'. I felt embarrassed that I am known to be such a greedy pig but I was still glad I got two!

For the palhe:

1 cup mahaar dhal 2 pieces (split urid beans)

1 teaspoon cumin seeds

1 teaspoon salt

1 teaspoon grated fresh root ginger (not
    frozen)

oil, for deep-frying

To serve:

¾ x 500 g carton natural set low-fat yogurt

milk

½ teaspoon red chilli powder

½ teaspoon garam masala

a handful of chopped fresh coriander

1 Leave the dhal in a pan of water to soak overnight.

2 The next day, rub the dhal with your hands to remove most of the skins. Rinse under the tap several times to remove the skins.

3 Place the dhal in a blender and whizz till smooth.

4 Mix with the cumin seeds, salt and ginger with a fork.

5 Divide into small balls and flatten slightly.

6 Heat the oil to about 170°C, or until a drop of the mixture rises to the surface at once. Deep-fry the *palhe* until golden. Drain on kitchen paper and leave to cool for 2 hours.

7 Place in a bowl of boiling water and leave to soak for 10 minutes.

8 Mix the yogurt with enough milk to make a smooth mixture.

9 Squeeze all the water out of the *palhe* and add to the yogurt.

10 Garnish with the chilli powder, garam masala and a handful of coriander.

On next page: my Dad and Sant Baba Kulwant Singh Ji at the *Gurudwara*

Akhand Path

This ceremony can be used to mark occasions

such as births, deaths and birthdays.

A continuous recitation of the

Guru Granth Sahib by five readers

for 48 hours is called Akhand Path

(incessant recitation by relays).

This is read by a Granthi, who is respected in

the community as a reader of the

Guru Granth Sahib.

SIMPLE LEMON ACHAAR

Once you have tasted this you will never want to eat another shop-bought pickle again. The lemon marinates itself with the ginger and you are left with soft tangy lemons that are a delight to eat with *roti.*

8 lemons, cut into 12 pieces

450 g (1 lb) fresh root ginger, peeled and cut in
  small pieces

5 tablespoons salt

1 teaspoon ground turmeric

½ teaspoon red chilli powder

1 Place the lemons and ginger in a large bowl and add the rest of the ingredients. Stir well.

2 Place in a large jar and close very tightly. Leave unopened for 10 days but tip the jar upside-down occasionally to mix.

ADDICTIVE LEMON AND RED CHILLI ACHAAR

This is lemon pickle taken to another level. The bright yellow lemons are mixed with pickling spices and scarlet chillies to create a pickle to die for. This was served at the *Akhand Path* of my cousin Jasneal and, after eating it with my two *rotia*, I asked my Mum to ask for another one for me – I was so embarrassed being that greedy in a *Gurudwara* but I couldn't help myself, it was the *achaar's* fault!

4 teaspoons oil

2 teaspoons achaar mix

1 teaspoon ground turmeric

5 tablespoons salt

8 lemons, each cut into 12 pieces

450 g (1 lb) fresh root ginger, peeled and cut into small pieces

6 large red chillies, halved lengthways

1 Heat the oil on a very, very low heat and add the achaar mix, turmeric and salt. Stir well.

2 Add the lemons, ginger and chillies and stir thoroughly.

3 Leave to cool.

4 Place in a large jar and leave unopened for 10 days, tipping upside-down occasionally to mix.

APPLE ACHAAR

Regular eating apples do not really work in this *achaar*; you need to use a cooking apple for the right texture and level of sourness. This is a lovely unusual pickle that is perfect eaten with any dhal, *rotia* or *parathe*.

3 tablespoons oil	1 teaspoon salt
2 teaspoons achaar mix	2 teaspoons sugar
1 onion, sliced	7 green chillies, sliced
¼ teaspoon ground turmeric	1 large cooking apple, sliced thinly

1 Heat the oil and add the achaar mix.

2 Add the onion and fry until the onion is soft.

3 Add the turmeric, salt, sugar, chillies and apple. Fry until the apple is cooked. Leave to cool.

4 Place in a container and refrigerate. Eat within 1 week.

Gajara di achaar
CARROT PICKLE

A true Punjabi pickle, this adds a little crunch to your meal. I love eating this with any *sabji* and especially love it with *dhalwala parathe* (page 164) and *dahi*. With its bright orange colour, it is also a colourful addition to any table.

3 tablespoons oil

2 teaspoons achaar mix

¼ teaspoon ground turmeric

1 teaspoon salt

2 teaspoons sugar

6 carrots, peeled and cut in thin batons

2 tablespoons lemon juice

1 Heat the oil and add the achaar mix, turmeric, salt and sugar. Stir well.

2 Add the carrots and stir-fry for 3 minutes. Turn off the heat and stir in the lemon juice. Leave to cool.

3 Place in a container and refrigerate. Eat within 1 week.

My sister Karen and I making *samose*

old skool

DISHES AND TECHNIQUES

Khadhi

(kah-ree)

POTATOES AND ONIONS IN A GRAM FLOUR, YOGURT AND FENUGREEK SAUCE

I have to admit that I have a real problem with the word 'curry'. Neither Indians nor British Asians use this word. This word instinctively makes me think of the days of the British Raj in India. A time when any English dish that had a bit of chilli added to it was passed off as Indian food and anything, be it fish, vegetable, meat, was all curry. These concoctions were about as authentically Indian as Coronation Chicken. And curry powder? What is that all about? It was invented by the Colonials in Madras to export to England and is certainly not a blend I have ever tasted in authentic Indian food.

I also grew up very confused about curry sauce in chip shops. I am still not sure what it is made of, have not uncovered the tenuous link to Indian food and am not quite sure why it is there amongst the haddock and pickled eggs of such an English establishment, but I like it. Its soft sweetness and velvety texture was always comforting on my walk home from school. Therefore, there is a real use of the word 'curry' in this country and still no one really knows where the word originates from. There are many theories, one of them being that it comes from the name of this dish. The very idea breaks my heart as this, out of all the recipes in this book, is my ultimate favourite. Its seductive, thick, tangy, bright yellow, gram flour, yogurt, lemon and fenugreek sauce with chunks of soft potato and onion couldn't be further away from the pale brown curry in freezer compartments in the local supermarket. I am so enamoured with this Punjabi dish par excellence that I refrained from learning how to make it until very recently. I wanted to retain the mystery of it all. My Mum is the only person who makes it just how I like it and I love seeing it appear on the table. Because it takes a lot of time and constant attention, I am only treated to it occasionally (sometimes I have to bribe my Mum, like, clean the whole house in return, or sometimes I just get it as a treat when she is in a good mood). The recipe is a very old one and is one of those dishes that the younger generation are not cooking as much. That is a shame as this original vegetarian speciality should not be lost.

Some people also add cooked pakore to the khadhi right at the end of cooking but, whichever way you make it, it goes with Rice with Onion, Peas and Cumin (page 148) like fish goes with chips.

20 ml (1 tablespoon + 1 teaspoon) oil

1 onion, halved lengthways, halved again and
   then cut into slices widthways

2 garlic cloves, chopped finely

1 tablespoon fenugreek seeds

1 tablespoon cumin seeds

⅓ cup canned chopped tomatoes, whizzed in
   a blender

500 g carton of natural set low-fat yogurt

1 cup gram flour

3 green chillies, chopped finely

2 teaspoons frozen grated fresh root ginger

2 teaspoons salt

2 teaspoons ground turmeric

2 teaspoons garam masala

a large handful of chopped fresh coriander

2 teaspoons citric acid

4 potatoes, peeled and quartered

1 Heat the oil in a very large saucepan – the sauce bubbles up quite high so it needs the room – and add the onion and garlic.

2 When the onions have softened, add the fenugreek and cumin seeds. Stir well.

3 Fry on a very low heat until the onions are soft and have been coloured by the cumin seeds.

4 Add the tomatoes and stir well to blend together.

5 Place the yogurt in a mixing bowl or pan and mix with ¾ cup of water to a smooth consistency. Sieve in the gram flour or pour it in and remove the lumps with your hands. Whisk until smooth.

6 Stir the onion and tomato mixture and press down with the spoon to crush the onions into the tomato. Add the chilli, ginger, salt, turmeric and garam masala.

7 Stir well to create a paste, adding splashes of water if necessary. Add the coriander.

8 Stir in the yogurt mixture and stir thoroughly.

9 Turn the heat up to medium.

10 Add 6 cups of cold water and the citric acid and bring to the boil, stirring occasionally.

11 Turn down to a simmer. Once the mixture settles down, turn the heat up very slightly.

12 Partly cover and simmer for 30 minutes, stirring every 5 minutes.

13 Add the potatoes and stir.

14 Partly cover again and simmer for another 30 minutes.

Sarson da saag

(sa-rohn-dha saag)
PURÉED MUSTARD LEAVES

Of all the Punjabi dishes, this is the most famous and is craved all over India and in the UK. Its name can be roughly translated as 'puréed mustard leaves' but it can be made with most green leafy vegetables, such as rapeseed leaves or spring cabbage. As it takes such a long time to cook and an unbelievable amount of bicep power (slightly alleviated here by the use of a hand mixer) it is thoroughly appreciated when it is lovingly ladled, steaming hot, on to your plate with makhi di roti, butter, raw mooli and lemon achaar.

This is my brother Aneil's most favourite dish and my Dad has many a time looked longingly at the acidic yellow fields of rapeseed plants around the country, reminding him of the fields in his village in the Punjab. Actually, one time, it was taken a step further. When I was about 11, Papiji and my Dad actually stopped the car at one of those fields and scampered off, only to emerge a few minutes later with armfuls of the leaves, which they hurriedly stuffed into the boot. When they sat down to the wonderful dish later, they felt their act was entirely justified.

Most methods that involve cooking green leaves usually result in a boring, bland, watery dish. This is the one truly delicious way to eat your greens. It is very cheap to make and, as it is full of iron, it is extremely good for you – I am sure Popeye would have liked to have known about it. I have given here the traditional recipe, which can serve about 20 people, simply because this is the way it is made. You can reduce the quantities to suit (halve or quarter) or you can do what most families do and divide the cooked saag (without adding the tarka) into portions and freeze (it will keep for a month or so). Then when you want to eat the next portion, simply heat, make a fresh tarka and enjoy. When cooking, remember to be careful of the steam and each time you plunge the madhua in, turn the gas low and stand back so it doesn't splash into your face.

When my Pooiji was showing me how to make this, she explained about Punjabi life and why the food is the way it is. She told me that Punjabi men and women had a very tough, hardworking, rural lifestyle. They never sat down for a minute and their days were full of very physical tasks. The men would work in the fields, or at other manual labour, all day and the women would spend their days doing the housework and cooking for each mealtime. The men did not want to return from their labour, tired and sweaty to fanciful little dishes. They wanted hearty, simple, filling and wholesome food. The women

Traditional utensils used to make *Langar* (the temple meal) in the *Gurudwara* (temple)

made dishes that were full of flavour but which were practical, healthy and suited the busy lifestyle. Although there was a lot to be done in a day, teamwork was very important. Everyone did their share and no one had the time to become stressed, exhausted or depressed like so many people do today. Everyone shared burdens and therefore there was constant support, you knew you could rely on people and that you weren't alone. In fact, so close were these bonds that very often women would start producing milk if women close to them were having children. The women worked hard their whole lives until the daughter-in-law would enter the household and lift the responsibility from the older woman's shoulders. Cooking this wonderful *saag* would be one of the many tasks she would take over.

SERVES 20

8 bunches of any greens, e.g. brussels sprout tops, spring cabbage, rapeseed leaves, mustard leaves or spring greens, washed and finely sliced

12 teaspoons salt

1 kg (2¼ lb) frozen broccoli florets

794 g can of puréed palak (spinach)

a handful of finely chopped fenugreek leaves

⅓ cup grated fresh root ginger, (not frozen)

25 green chillies, chopped finely

4 teaspoons white sugar

1 cup fine corn flour (polenta)

1 cup coarse corn flour (polenta)

8 tablespoons oil

1 large onion, chopped finely

7 garlic cloves, chopped finely

butter, to serve

1 Get a large (about 8-litre/14-pint) pan. Fill it to halfway with cold water and bring to the boil.

2 Add the eight bunches of greens.

3 Add the salt, the broccoli and the spinach purée and gently pound the mixture into the water using a *madhua*.

4 Partly cover, with the heat on high, and bring to the boil.

5 Turn the heat down to a simmer and add the fenugreek leaves. Leave to simmer for 1 hour, pounding every 10 minutes to push the leaves into the water.

6 Add the ginger and chillies. Stir well. Switch off the heat.

7 Using a hand mixer that is plugged in near the hob, blend the mixture in the pan for 5 minutes. Stir well.

8 Put the heat back on to medium and partly cover. Simmer again for 1 more hour, pounding every 10 minutes.

9 Turn off the heat and blend again for 5 minutes. Add the sugar. The *saag* needs the power of the chilli but the sugar pacifies it slightly and takes the edge off it.

11 Leave uncovered to reduce any water.

12 Mix the two cups of corn flour together in a bowl. Add 2 cups of water and blend to a smooth paste with your fingers.

13 Turn the heat off again and, whilst blending again, slowly add the corn flour. Keep blending until it is thoroughly blended, even and smooth.

14 Turn the heat back on to very low and keep pounding every few minutes.

15 Pound well and leave for 15 minutes. Switch off the heat.

16 Heat the oil in a frying pan and add the onion and garlic. Fry until a deep golden brown and then stir well into the *saag*. Top with a good knob of butter.

Home-made dahi

(da-hee)

YOGURT

This is the very old and traditional method of making natural set yogurt. My Mum used to make it this way when I was younger but now we mostly buy cartons, like most other British-Asian households. I hope people do continue to occasionally make it this way, though, as it is such a lovely process and there is something very satisfying about making your own yogurt. It is also very economical as you can make a large quantity just from some milk. With most cartons from supermarkets costing about a pound, this is very cheap by comparison. Use your airing cupboard to achieve the right level of heat and moisture – just don't kick it over when you reach in there, all bleary-eyed, for a towel the next morning.

600 ml (1 pint) full-fat milk   **2 tablespoons natural set low-fat yogurt**

1 Bring the milk to the boil in a large saucepan. Leave to cool – about 1 hour.
2 Beat the yogurt with a fork and add to the milk.
3 Pour the mixture from one pan to another several times until a frothy surface appears.
4 Pour into a large plastic container, cover with a clean tea towel and leave overnight in the airing cupboard.

HOME-MADE GARAM MASALA

Garam masala is the only spice blend we really use in our home cooking and is therefore of vital importance. Nowadays a lot of British-Asian families use ready-ground garam masala from the Indian grocers. The only problem with this is that you often don't know what ingredients have been used. As some people's stomachs are sensitive to some of the spices, the best way to get around it is to make your own. This is the garam masala that my Mum makes and the smell of the spices slowly roasting away permeating around the house is one of life's purest pleasures.

2 kg (4½ lb) coriander seeds

500 g (1 lb 2 oz) black peppercorns

2 kg (4½ lb) cumin seeds

250 g (9 oz) cassia bark

100 g (3½ oz) large brown cardamoms

a handful of bay leaves

100 g (3½ oz) cloves

1 Make sure you thoroughly wash all the spices in running cold water using a sieve before roasting.

2 Place the ingredients evenly on a piece of foil on a baking tray or grill pan. Roast gently in an oven at 160°C/fan oven 140°C/Gas Mark 3 or under a very low grill until dry and roasted, turning over occasionally with a fork. When you can run a fork through the spices and none of them stick to it then you know they are bone dry and ready to be cooled and then ground.

3 Leave to cool and then grind to a powder. Use a clean coffee grinder (you don't want coffee-tasting garam masala or garam-masala-tasting coffee).

4 When ground, store in an airtight container and place somewhere dry, dark and cool. It should keep up to 6 months.

(pee-nah) *pina*

DRINKS

Nimbu pani

(neem-boo-paa-nee)

LEMONADE

This is the refreshing thirst-quencher sold on the streets of India. It is just what you need on a hot summer's day, when regular soft drinks just aren't doing the business. The sourness of the lemon goes well with the pepper and cumin flavours that circulate throughout the glass.

SERVES 1

¼ teaspoon cumin seeds

juice of 1 lemon

2 teaspoons sugar

¼ teaspoon salt

freshly ground black pepper

1 Place the cumin seeds in a dry frying pan and gently roast. Leave to cool. Crush in a pestle and mortar.

2 Take a large glass of water with ice cubes. Add the lemon juice, sugar, salt, a grind of black pepper and cumin and stir well. Serve chilled.

LASSI

Everyone loves a cool *lassi*, but I hate the type that is made so thick that you may as well eat it with a spoon. The variations I give here are cool and refreshing and totally hit the spot. I often make my own right there and then at the table, by adding a few spoons of *dahi* to my glass of water and stirring furiously to mix. Pour into a large tumbler over lots of ice cubes and serve with a sprig of mint or two.

SERVES 1

For a salty lassi:

1 glass of water

3 tablespoons natural set low-fat yogurt

1/3 cup milk

1/2 teaspoon salt

1/2 teaspoon garam masala

For a sweet lassi:

1 glass of water

3 tablespoons natural set low-fat yogurt

1/3 cup milk

2 teaspoons sugar

For a pistachio lassi:

1 glass of water

3 tablespoons natural set low-fat yogurt

1/4 cup chopped pistachios

2 teaspoons sugar

Whizz all the ingredients in a blender and serve over ice.

Elaichi chaa

(lejj-ee-chaah)

INDIAN CARDAMOM TEA

This is the one thing that most British-Asian girls get asked to make but they either don't know how or have forgotten how to. Picture the scene if you will, see if it sounds familiar. Imagine… you're at a relative's house and your Mum has popped to the shops with some distant twice-removed **Massiji** (aunt) to pick up some coriander from the Indian grocers next to the gold shop – they'll be at least four hours. You're left minding all the snotty-nosed little brat children and suddenly an elderly **Auntyji** turns to you, pulls your left cheek and with a toothless grin asks you to make her some Indian tea like a good little girl.

You have been spending more time listening to garage than being in the kitchen, despite your mother's desperate pleas. You have often thought that to spend a Saturday afternoon in a kitchen being taught how to make **aloo gobi** is a pastime only reserved for the truly socially hopeless **pindhus**. You have friends to meet, essays to complete, clothes to buy, hair to highlight, ring-tones to download and texting techniques to be perfected. Exasperated as your parents may be, you are happy with a life that is filled with **bhangra** not **bhajis**, daytimers not dhal, Moschino not mooli and diamante tikkas not chicken **tikkas**.

Yet here you are, stuck in this semi-detached in Bradford on a Sunday evening confronted by a slightly cross-eyed creature in a pale green floral Indian suit and brown cardigan with tennis socks poking from leather toe-thong sandals asking for **elaichi** tea, and there's nowhere to run. You are going to have to somehow make this damn tea and your Mum has left her mobile in her bag tucked beside the sofa. You also know fully well that if you fail, not only will your **Mummyji** give you a front and backhanded slap when she returns but the **Auntyji** will wail to the entire Indian community (India and Canada included along with the UK) that you are an absolute disgrace of an Indian girl and a shame to your mother. So here's how to make it just how they like it so this doesn't happen to you again. Sweet and milky, just remember to serve with a plate of assorted biscuits.

3 green cardamom pods

2 brown cardamom pods

2 teabags

4 tablespoons sugar

milk

1 Put about 7 cups of fresh cold water in a large saucepan.
2 Lightly smash the cardamoms in a pestle and mortar. Add to the water.
3 Bring to the boil.
4 When boiling, add the teabags and sugar.
5 Add enough milk to turn it a pale beige colour.
6 Bring to the boil again and just as it is rising to the top of the pan, switch off the heat.
7 Pour through a strainer.

POMEGRANATE SYRUP MILKSHAKE

Pomegranate syrup is available from all Indian grocery stores and is well worth keeping a bottle in the cupboard. This is a rich variant of the classic milkshake and will be unlike anything you've ever tasted.

SERVES 1

pomegranate syrup

milk

vanilla ice cream

1 Mix 1 part of pomegranate syrup to 5 parts of milk and stir well.
2 Top with a dollop of vanilla ice cream.

SPICED ORANGE JUICE

The garam masala, pepper and cinnamon heighten the citrus taste of the juice and simply add to the pleasure. My Chachaji used to drink this with a raw egg in it, which used to totally gross me out, so I'll stick to the version without. Feel free to add an egg if you wish, though.

SERVES 1

a glass of freshly squeezed orange juice

a pinch of salt

a pinch of garam masala

a pinch of freshly ground black pepper

a pinch of ground cinnamon

a fresh mint sprig

1 Add the salt, garam masala, pepper and cinnamon to the orange juice and stir well.
2 Garnish with the mint.

STRAWBERRY, MANGO AND ROSE-WATER SMOOTHIE

Blushing strawberries and amber mangoes are the ideal base for a smoothie. Add some hedonistic raspberry ripple ice cream and a dash of Eastern rose-water and you have transformed the simple smoothie into a drink far more luxurious.

SERVES 2

4 strawberries

1 cup mango juice

2 scoops raspberry ripple ice cream

4 drops of rose-water

Whizz all the ingredients in a blender until smooth and frothy.

RASPBERRY SHARBART

Sharbarts are served in India on special occasions and in the hot blazing heat of summer. I have used raspberries to make this version, which makes a beautiful fuchsia-coloured drink at summer garden parties or barbecues. Serve the crushed frozen *sharbart* over the puréed raspberries in large glasses and top with fresh mint, adding elegant straws if you wish, or serve it all in a large jug garnished with whole raspberries.

SERVES 2

½ cup raspberries

2 teaspoons lime juice

2 tablespoons caster sugar

2 cups of water

a few drops of rose-water

1 cup of raspberries, puréed in a blender, to serve

fresh mint sprigs, to garnish

1 Whizz the raspberries, lime juice, sugar, water and rose-water in a blender. Place in a container and freeze.

2 Lightly thaw and crush the frozen *sharbart* to create the texture of a slush puppy.

3 Serve over puréed raspberries, garnished with mint sprigs.

BOMBAYLLINIS

Based on the Bellini, this version adds an exotic charm to the glitzy tipple. Perfect for parties; serve with Dry Masala Mixed Nuts (page 65) and other snacks to be the hostess with the mostest.

SERVES 8 – 10

1 large mango, peeled and stoned

1 bottle of Champagne

slivers of mango, to garnish

1 Purée the mango in a blender.

2 Divide the purée amongst champagne glasses, and top with champagne. You need roughly a third mango purée to two-thirds champagne.

3 Garnish with a sliver of mango.

COLA AND MILK

You've got to believe me on this one. British Asians have been drinking this since the seventies, usually in summer. When I was little I thought it was a version of tea for children, as that's what it looked like. Beige in colour, it was served in little glasses and I loved its creamy sweetness. I was in my teens when, after a conversation with my friend on the way home from school, I discovered non-Asian people didn't drink it and thought it sounded like the most disgusting thing ever created on this planet. Trust me, it really is wonderful, just make sure the cola and milk are cold and that the cola goes in first. You can also serve it over ice.

SERVES 1

good quality fizzy cola   **semi-skimmed milk**

1 Pour ¼ glass full of cola.
2 Top with milk, do not stir, and just drink.

WATERMELON AND LEMON COOLER

It's a hot day and you're sitting out in the garden, flies buzzing all around you and sweat dripping down the back of your neck. What you need is this drink to sooth your parched throat and refresh parts other drinks can't reach. The best summer drink in the world? Probably.

SERVES 1

1 large wedge of watermelon, peeled,   **juice of ½ lemon**
   de-seeded and cut in chunks   **1 teaspoon sugar**

Place in a blender and whizz till smooth.

INDIA

Mascat
Calcutta
Bombay
Kuria Muria
(Br.)
Hyderabad
Bay
Arabian
Goa
(Port)
Cocanada
Ben
Madras
Sea
cotra
Laccadive Mahé
(Fr.)
Pondicherry
I.s (Br.)
Negapatam (Fr.)
Nicobar
(B
Colombo
Maldive I.s
(Br.)
I N D D I A
Equator
Equator

mittha *(mi-taah)*

SWEETS

Gajarela

(gaj-a-reh-la)

SWEET CARROT DESSERT

Westerners eat carrot cake; we from the East eat *gajarela* or carrot halva as it is also known. This bright orange dish captures all the inherent sweetness of the carrots, harnessing them with cloves, cardamom and cinnamon to create a moist, gleaming speciality eaten on Diwali and other special occasions.

SERVES 4 — 6

10 large carrots, peeled and grated

7 tablespoons butter

5 cloves

6 green cardamoms, crushed

a small piece of cinnamon stick

¼ cup milk

½ cup granulated sugar

1 Bring a pan of water to the boil. Add the carrots and simmer for 10 minutes. Drain into a colander.

2 Melt the butter in a pan with the cloves, cardamom and cinnamon on a very low heat.

3 Add the milk and stir well.

4 When you can smell the cardamom, add the sugar.

5 Stir until the sugar has dissolved and then add the carrots.

6 Gently stir until the liquid has dried.

7 Cover and cook on a very low heat for 15 minutes.

DRESSED WATERMELON

I have just read an article in a magazine that recommended eating fresh strawberries with balsamic vinegar. This is based upon the same principle as this fruit dessert. Indians have long known that adding a little salt, spice or a sour ingredient to fruit really brings out all its sweetness. I have grown up watching my *Papiji* and my Dad eating apples, oranges and mangoes sprinkled with salt and pepper but it is the combination of salt, garam masala and cumin on crimson watermelon, heavy with all its juice, that I love the most.

SERVES 4 – 6

1 teaspoon cumin seeds

1 teaspoon garam masala

½ teaspoon salt

1 large slice of watermelon per person, cut into chunks

1 In a dry frying pan, roast the cumin seeds. Leave to cool
2 Crush the cumin seeds in a pestle and mortar.
3 Mix with the salt and garam masala.
4 Sprinkle the mixture over the watermelon and serve.

Kheer

RICE PUDDING

This lovely milky rice pudding with cardamom and rose-water is often served as part of a wedding meal and was one of the things Indian girls used to learn to cook before they got married.

SERVES 10

1 cup basmati rice, washed

2.25 litres (4 pints) full-fat milk

10 green cardamoms, crushed

¼ cup flaked almonds

2 cups white sugar

a few drops of rose-water

1 Take a very large pan (about a 4-litre/7-pint capacity – it needs to be big as the milk boils up) and add 1.2 litres (2 pints) of water. Bring to the boil.

2 Add the rice and stir for 30 minutes until the rice looks as though it is beginning to mash.

3 Add all the milk and, when it begins to boil, lower the heat. Keep stirring, so it doesn't stick, for 30 minutes.

4 After 30 minutes, add the cardamoms and almonds. Cook, stirring, for another 30 minutes.

5 After a total cooking time of 1 hour, when the mixture becomes thick, add the sugar. Turn the heat off and add the rose-water.

6 Serve immediately or refrigerate and serve cold.

Sevian

(se-vee-aan)

MILKY VERMICELLI

I have eaten this at weddings, mixed with ice cream into a sort of pink milkshake that we call *falooda*. In Turkey, they cook it with sweet sugar syrup and serve with crushed walnuts. This version is soft and creamy, with the noodles gently cooked in milk, rose syrup and rose-water. It is eaten hot from the pan or served cold with vanilla ice cream.

SERVES 8

600 ml (1 pint) full-fat milk

2 balls of dried vermicelli noodles

¾ cup white sugar

2 tablespoons rose syrup

a few drops of rose-water

a pinch of takmuria seeds

1 Pour the milk into a large saucepan and bring to the boil.

2 When boiling, add the vermicelli, which should be slightly broken. Lower the heat and keep stirring.

3 When the noodles are soft and the milk has thickened but is still thin enough to be a sauce, add the sugar and rose syrup. After a couple of minutes switch the heat off (the whole cooking time should be about 30 minutes). The noodles should still have a slight bite and there should still be some sauce.

4 Sprinkle with the rose water and takmuria. Serve warm or refrigerate and serve with vanilla ice cream.

Karaa

(ka-raah)

SWEET SEMOLINA

This sweet, thick, smooth dessert is similar to the *Parshad* (a sweetmeat we receive with thanks from the priests) that we have at the *Gurudwara*. This version is sprinkled with flaked almonds to give a little texture to this traditional home-made treat.

SERVES 4 – 6

½ cup butter

½ cup coarse semolina

½ cup sugar

¼ cup flaked almonds, broken up roughly

1 Melt the butter in a large saucepan on a very low heat.

2 Add the semolina and slowly mix in.

3 When it has become slightly gold, after about 15–20 minutes, switch the heat off. Add the sugar and stir.

4 Add 4 cups of water and turn the heat to very high. Stirring all the while, start to turn the heat lower as the mixture gets thicker; add extra splashes of water if needed.

5 When it is of a nice thick consistency, switch the heat off and sprinkle with the almonds.

Karah Parshad

At the end of a prayer ceremony,

the Karah Parshad is distributed

as a grace from the lord to all those present.

It is prepared from equal weights of sugar,

flour, water and butter.

Semolina is heated with butter

and hot sweetened water is added.

It is then all stirred together

to form a thick sweet dough.

Small amounts are placed into

the cupped palms of the devotees.

The person who prepares this offering

takes a bath before doing so and

repeats the five Sikh prayers whilst preparing it.

Zarda

(jarr-daa)

SWEET RICE

This is a gorgeous deep yellow basmati rice dish heavily laden with sugar, butter, cloves, cardamom, green sultanas and almonds. It is quite difficult to get right, some people make it too milky, some too dry and sugary and some add too much butter. When made just right, like the recipe below, it is a magical and fragrant dish and has a rather Arabian Nights feel to it. Eat it hot and steaming in little glass cups.

SERVES 4 – 6

1½ cups basmati rice

a few strands of saffron or yellow food colour

7 tablespoons butter

5 cloves

6 green cardamoms, crushed

¼ cup full-fat milk

1½ cups white sugar

a handful of green sultanas or golden sultanas

a handful of flaked almonds

1 Wash the rice and leave to soak in water for 30 minutes.

2 Place in a saucepan and fill to three-quarters full with water. Stir in the saffron or food colouring. Bring to the boil.

3 Simmer for 10 minutes, leaving it still slightly underdone. Drain into a colander immediately.

4 Heat the butter in a large saucepan on a very, very low heat. Add the cloves and cardamoms and stir well. Add the milk and stir. When you can smell the cardamom, add the sugar.

5 Stir until the sugar has dissolved and you have a smooth paste.

6 Add the rice. Do not stir but use a palette knife to push the rice from one side of the pan to the other until all the liquid has dried. Be careful not to break any of the rice grains.

7 When there is no liquid left but the rice is still moist, sprinkle on the sultanas and almonds.

8 Place three sheets of kitchen paper, one on top of the other, on top of the pan. Place the lid over the kitchen paper and continue to cook on a very, very low heat for about 15 minutes.

POMEGRANATE RUBIES WITH LIME

Pomegranates are indeed captivating. The way the hard skin protects the dazzling
jewels inside, revealed by persevering through layers of yellow pith, is extraordinary.
This dessert celebrates those little gems by creating a spiced cascade of them over
passion-fruit and cardamom ice cubes, which is then topped with cream and juicy lime.
This is a contemporary sweet, which looks and tastes sophisticated and stylish.

SERVES 2

6 green cardamom pods

1 small carton of passion-fruit juice

2 cups of pomegranate kernels (about 2
   pomegranates)

a pinch of salt

a pinch of garam masala

4 tablespoons single cream

2 twists of lime

1 Place a pod of cardamom in each of six compartments in an ice-cube tray and fill
each with passion-fruit juice. Freeze for about 2 hours.

2 Place three ice cubes in each of two large wine glasses.

3 Top each with a cup of pomegranate kernels.

4 Add a pinch of salt and garam masala to each and spoon 2 tablespoons of cream
over each glass. Garnish with a twist of lime.

Beautiful statues of Hindu Gods

ROASTED FRUIT WRAPS

This is quite unusual but involves heating the fruit through with a little sugar and then creating little wraps with crème fraîche, rose-water and crushed pistachios. Served chilled, the result is quite a rainbow of flavours.

SERVES 2

½ mango, peeled and sliced thinly

1 peach, halved, stoned and sliced thinly

1 kiwi fruit, sliced

8 raspberries

a sprinkle of sugar

2 tortilla wraps

4 tablespoons crème fraîche

4 drops of rose-water

a handful of chopped pistachios

1 Preheat the oven to 200°C/fan oven 180°C/Gas Mark 6. Spread the fruit evenly on a piece of foil on a baking tray.

2 Sprinkle with sugar and bake in the oven for 8 minutes.

3 Divide the fruit between the two wraps, add 2 tablespoons of crème fraîche to each, wrap and sprinkle on a couple of drops of the rose-water and some pistachios.

4 Fold the wraps up by folding the bottom inwards and then the two sides into the middle.

5 Refrigerate for 30 minutes before serving.

MENU PLANNERS

Some dishes just simply have their natural partners: bangers and mash, beans on toast, fish and chips, spaghetti bolognaise and so on. The first six in the menu plans below are exactly like that. They are traditional complete meals just the way we eat them at home – a bit of a ritual actually! For *saag* goes hand in hand with *makhi di roti; aloo parathe* just won't do without *dahi* and *gajar achaar* and where would *khadhi* be without Rice with onion, peas and cumin? Eat them like this and you will experience a truly authentic, home-style culinary delight. The remaining menu plans are dishes which do not go together quite so strictly but complement each other in terms of flavour and texture, provide perfect balanced meals and are therefore eaten in these combinations often. Enjoy!

Sarson da saag
(puréed mustard leaves), page 193
Makhi di roti (cornflour bread),
page 163
Dahi (natural yogurt), page 196
Mooli (white radish)
Addictive lemon and red chilli achaar,
page 185
Karaa (sweet semolina), page 215
Salty *lassi*, page 201

My Mum's *thariwala* chicken, page 106
Special mixed vegetable rice, page 152
Saaf di masoor dhal
(whole brown/green lentils), page 99
Tharwala dahi (cucumber yogurt),
page 175
Gajarela (sweet carrot dessert),
page 211
Watermelon and lemon cooler, page 206

Aloo paratha, page 164
Dahi (natural yogurt), page 196
Gajara di achaar (carrot pickle),
page 187
Sevian (milky vermicelli), page 214
Sweet *lassi*, page 201

ACKNOWLEDGEMENTS
To God I simply offer my humble
thanks.

Thank you to my ancestors
whose amazing talents and recipes
have found their way to me through
the trickle of time.

A lifetime of thanks to my
parents, brother Aneil and sister
Karen. Thank you for your support
and all the laughter.

Many, many thanks to all of my
relatives, for all you have taught me
over the years, your kindness and for
being such a source of inspiration.
Many thanks to all who agreed to
take part in the shoot.

Thank you to all my friends for
your absolute enthusiasm and for
keeping me sane!

Thank you to Angela Jordan for
being nothing short of my guardian
angel. A special thanks to my editor
extraordinaire, Susanna Clarke, and
the wonderful Janet Copleston, at
Simon and Schuster for having such
vision and for having faith in me.

Thank you to Rosemary Scoular
for all your advice and support, it has
been invaluable and so very much
appreciated.

A big thank you to Mammaji and
Mammiji for allowing us to shoot at
the Gurudwara. A special mention
to Aneil who is so brave with PWS.
Please may I urge you all to visit
www.pwsa.co.uk.

Also thanks to Deborah Savage
for your meticulous editing; Jane
Humphrey and Kate Miller for their
beautiful work; Mark Luscombe-
Whyte; James Kellow, Rachael
Healey and Sue Stephens; the
extremely talented creative team,
Ben Stafford and Chris Harris,
Stewart Howard for inspiring me to
write; Lynne, Cat, Pete, IT and
everyone at Tequila Ad agency;
everyone at the Society of Authors;
Zadie Smith for the good luck
charm; Annabel Wright; Mark
Jackson.